THE tugutil

THE TRUE STORY OF GOD'S LIFE-CHANGING WORK
AMONG THE TUGUTIL PEOPLE OF INDONESIA

JOHN & BETTY SHARPE

The Tugutil
The true story of God's life-changing work among the Tugutil people of Indonesia

Copyright © 2015 by John and Betty Sharpe
Email: thetugutil@gmail.com

All Rights Reserved. Except as may be permitted by the Copyright Act, no part of this publication may be reproduced in any form or by any means without prior permission from the publisher.

Published by AccessTruth
PO Box 8087
Baulkham Hills NSW 2153
Australia
Email: info@accesstruth.com
Web: accesstruth.com

Unless otherwise indicated, Scripture quotations are from the ESV® Bible (The Holy Bible, English Standard Version®), copyright © 2001 by Crossway, a publishing ministry of Good News Publishers. Used by permission. All rights reserved.

Scripture marked 'NIV' taken from the Holy Bible, NEW INTERNATIONAL VERSION®, NIV® Copyright © 1973, 1978, 1984, 2011 by Biblica, Inc.® Used by permission. All rights reserved worldwide.

ISBN: 978-0-646-93959-9

Cover Photo is of Ula Ula, a much loved neighbour and dear friend of John and Betty who tragically died and never heard the story that they had come to tell.

Cover design and page layout by Matthew Hillier

"This book is an amazing testimony of both the power of the gospel and how God used John and Betty Sharpe for his glory among the Tugutil people.
There is one extraordinary story after another that keeps you riveted to each page. You come away wishing you were there and inspired to share Christ.
It's packed with gospel wisdom on how to do cross-cultural ministry. I found myself falling in love with the Tugutil people whom I'm so looking forward to meeting in the age to come. This is a must read!"

Ray Galea, Author and Senior Pastor at MBM Rooty Hill, Sydney

"The sacrifices, the highs and lows of mission service, the tears mixed with the joys of attempting to break into an unengaged culture, the privilege of watching firsthand, as God bursts into the lives of the Tugutil people. This was the experience of John and Betty and their little family as they ministered in the dense jungles of Indonesia. This is a must read account of reaching the unreached with the Gospel.
Read it, and be prepared to be used by God to reach your world today with the same message that transformed the Tugutil.
Thank you John and Betty for both your service and your honesty in your writing."

Keith Henderson, Chairman of CrossView Australia

"You'll be greatly blessed to read about God's amazing grace to the Tugutil people in one of the world's most remote corners. This story of our long-time friends, John and Betty, blended together with the story of the birth of the Tugutil church, is one that illustrates the incredible way that God uses his children to accomplish the difficult, the challenging… and even the impossible - if they will just simply trust him and follow him step by step into the unknown. By the end of the book you'll be so looking forward to the day you will meet your Tugutil family gathered around the Throne."

Larry Goring, Coordinator for International Ministries, NTM/Global Partners

"Reading this book is dangerous for people living a no-risk, comfortable life. This book will astound and challenge even the most adventurous, faith filled pioneers of this generation. As I read this story, I found myself saying time and time again, 'You must be kidding!'

It will make you (as it did me) ask 'have I been too safe, too comfortable, too in control?'

What John, Betty and their children did in the 1980's in the middle of the Indonesian jungle without the resources we have today, is a massive eye opener for a generation where comfort, safety and avoiding risk (especially with our children) often determines what we will and won't do for God.

The book was a joy to read. John is a masterful storyteller. He writes just as he speaks, with great humility and always giving honor to the great God that he and Betty love so much."

Paul Butler, Senior Pastor at New Heart Baptist, Brisbane
Proudly John and Betty's sending, supporting church family since 1976

CONTENTS

Foreword..9
1. The Long Journey to Lili...13
2. Indonesia, Here We Come...19
3. Living in Pontianak..23
4. More Tales From Pontianak..29
5. The Move to North Maluku..33
6. The Survey Trip..39
7. Maybe Those Stories Were True...................................45
8. Under Attack..49
9. The Sinking...55
10. Fire on Our Boat..65
11. Fredi's Story..71
12. 'Happy the Way They Are'..73
13. The 'Tokatas'...79
14. Will We Ever Get This Language?..............................83
15. Building the Airstrip..87
16. The Hardest Thing...91
17. Our Undependable Airstrip..95
18. Challenges and Discouragement................................99
19. The Deadly Measles Epidemic..................................101
20. Our Medical Program Dilemma..............................105
21. Church - the Strongest Taboo...................................109
22. Can They Hear Us?..113
23. The Transformation Begins......................................117
24. Not Academy Award Calibre, but They Got the Point...121
25. O Toro's Death..125

26. In the Middle of a Spiritual Battle..131
27. Giving of the Law..135
28. Fun Moments During the Teaching.......................................139
29. The Story Draws to a Close...143
30. More Fun With Our Tugutil Friends......................................147
31. Betty's Story of Little Israel..151
32. Singing, a Wonderful New Experience for the Tugutil......161
33. Etanga's Story...165
34. The First Baptisms...169
35. Reflecting on the Experience..173

We dedicate this book to our three wonderful children Naomi, Anita and Matthew, their spouses and to our precious grandchildren. May it inspire them to follow Christ unreservedly and have a heart for the most marginalised people of this world.

ACKNOWLEDGEMENTS

A special thank you to Ally Chumley who freely offered many hours of service in editing the rough manuscript into a very readable form. Also to our team of proof readers, who at various stages of the book's development, poured over it, further refining it. To Ernestine Beckers, Karen Bland, David Whittaker and Kym Dickman, a huge thank you to each one of you for your contribution to the finished manuscript. We also want to especially thank Matthew Hillier who did absolutely everything else necessary to see the final product presented, printed and distributed. What a pleasure it has been to work with such a wonderful team of people.

FOREWORD

Declare His glory among the nations, His marvellous works among all the peoples!

PSALM 96:3 (NIV)

The period during which we lived among the Tugutil people of Indonesia involved some extraordinarily difficult times, yet also yielded the most rewarding, fascinating and faith-building episodes one could ever experience. On numerous occasions, as we shared stories of our years among these amazing people, we were strongly encouraged to put them together in a book. One man who was particularly insistent that the story be written was my mentor Ray Galea, who made writing a chapter of the story a condition for each time we met together.

The story you are about to read is based on our recollections of events and the many letters Betty wrote to our dear families, friends and the many wonderful people who gave financially to the ministry, enabling us to be there. Many of those people faithfully prayed for our safety and for the Tugutil people, and God obviously answered those prayers. One couple who did an outstanding job of faithfully keeping our needs before our sending church in Brisbane were David and Sandra Evans. They visited us in Indonesia and constantly looked out for us, always encouraging others to do likewise.

Of course, for some people, the very idea of missionaries seeking to 'convert' tribal people to another belief system is rather offensive. My boss at my last place of employment felt that way and just before heading off to Bible College, asked me why we couldn't just leave them alone. 'After all,' he insisted, 'they're happy the way they are.'

Our story certainly exposes that myth for what it is. The most powerful testament to this came when a young anthropologist moved into the area and told one of our tribal men that many people back in the United States believed that we missionaries had done the tribal people a great disservice. He explained how his American friends believed that the Tugutil were actually much better off before we turned up and introduced them to the Christian Gospel. The young Tugutil man responded with a look of total disbelief. He then proceeded to describe just how difficult and fear-filled tribal life was prior to our coming. He then challenged the anthropologist to invite those who held that belief to come and live just the way the Tugutil did prior to the coming of the Gospel, before God's transforming power altered their way of life. Maybe then these critics could also experience first-hand something of the misery and fear that was often the norm in Tugutil tribal life.

I'd like to acknowledge some other people who made this book possible, by the stories they shared during our time with the Tugutil and afterwards. These people were our faithful co-workers, Keith and Anita Miles; Don and Heather McCall; and Christianus and Otari Lahu. All of them could and probably should write their own books, individually documenting their amazing experiences. Years later, another family - Bob and Debbie Clark - would join

FOREWORD

Our Lili Team in 1982 (back row, left to right): Chris & Otari; Betty & John; Don & Heather; Anita & Keith (front row, left to right) Naomi & Anita; Esther & Rebecca; Kevin & Eric

the work and assist Keith's work towards the completion of the Bible translation project. At the time of writing, Bob Clark continues in the task of completing the Tobelorise New Testament, while Keith and Anita Miles continue to add to the many Old Testament books and portions they have translated. This amazing couple who unfortunately were back in the US during the initial sharing of the gospel story, regularly travel back into the tribe, often on rickety old boats, despite now being in their seventies. Poor health and numerous other obstacles haven't daunted their determination to unreservedly serve these people for whom they have a very special place in their hearts. That feeling is reciprocated by the tribal people and the many other Indonesians whom they have assisted and loved over the years they served in that country. Some of the photos included in the book were taken by Keith and we are so grateful for the visual record they now help provide.

Of course, the children from each of our families also have their own stories.

We can't talk about our team without including our many faithful Tugutil brothers and sisters and other wonderful Indonesian national workers who also became vital team members and God's servants to the Tugutil. Finally, the one aspect of this book which stands out above all else is the identity of the story's real hero. Undoubtedly, God alone takes that place. His love, grace and mercy to the Tugutil people, His desire that they hear His story and His amazing ability to change people's hearts and lives through His revealed Word, is the outstanding message that pervades all you're about to read.

- 1 -
THE LONG JOURNEY TO LILI

But seek first the kingdom of God and His righteousness,
and all these things will be added to you.

MATTHEW 6:33

When we married on January 4, 1975 at our little Presbyterian church in Brisbane, Betty and I had no idea that 13 months later we would be heading to Sydney to embark on three years of training to become overseas cross-cultural missionaries. After several weeks of married life, we began attending Rochedale Baptist church in Brisbane. There we met a couple who were working with NTM. Over the preceding years of my life as a Christian, I had developed some interest in missions. Upon hearing of the existence of numerous language groups who had no opportunity to hear the amazing message of Jesus that had so dramatically transformed her life, Betty was keen for us to change that situation for at least one of those unreached groups of people. At that time, we decided that we would commence missionary training immediately after Betty completed her third year of General Nursing training at the Princess Alexandra Hospital in December of 1975. At the same time I would leave my job of maintaining SSB radios for the lighthouse section of the Department of Transport.

THE TUGUTIL

As I recall the decision to leave our places of employment, I'm reminded of my question to the missionary representative to whom we had spoken about cross-cultural ministry. I asked him how missionary work was financed.

'By faith,' he answered.

'By what?' Came my immediate reply.

We certainly knew of the word 'faith' as it applies to how mankind finds acceptance with God, but we knew nothing about what he referred to as 'living by faith'. He seemed to be implying that we would actually be depending on God to supply all the finances we would require in this line of work. 'So don't this mob pay you a salary?' I inquired. The man went on to explain how it had worked for his family and how it was working for thousands of others, aligned with various other missionary societies, who were doing the kind of thing we were considering doing. He then explained about a trip on which he was about to embark that would take him away from home for about a month. He had $60 in cash and a tankful of petrol, but believed that God would somehow meet all his needs. *This*, I thought with some scepticism, *will be fascinating to watch*. And watch we did. To our amazement, we witnessed God provide for this man in remarkable ways. Since God did that for him, we figured, then He could also do it for us, if it was His will for us to be involved in this ministry.

Just prior to our wedding day, we had taken possession of the keys to a brand new, small three bedroom home that we (and the bank) had purchased in Underwood for $22,500. The decision to train for missions prevented us from getting taken up with accumulating furniture and all the other household items that can often absorb the thinking and finances of young couples. We borrowed some furniture, hung an old bedspread at our sliding glass front door to serve as a curtain, and generally got by with what we had. This allowed us to save all the money we would need to get us through our training years.

Having no real idea what awaited us in Sydney, we loaded a friend's truck with all the furniture we did have and headed off to the NTM Training Centre in Plumpton, Western Sydney. In 1976 the trip should have taken us about 18 hours. However, we arrived around 48 hours later, thanks to encounters with flooded roads and other mishaps. Our heavily laden truck fell victim to three flat tyres, two of which we changed en route. But the third flat left us with no spare tyre to use as a replacement. We had also towed a car trailer with Betty's little VW Beetle on board behind the truck. This addition to our convoy came in handy when we needed to get the last of our flat tyres to the next town for repair. We wondered to ourselves whether this disastrous trip was a foretaste of what awaited us in our future life as missionaries.

Finally, we arrived at the Mission's property. We were directed to a tiny two-roomed cabin with no bathroom or running water. Somehow, we managed to squash everything into the two small rooms and our new neighbours quickly clued us in as to how to function with no running tap water. This was achieved by purchasing a plastic drum with a tap and a couple of plastic bowls for washing up, similar to those campers use. I'm sure the leadership's reasoning at the time was to make the training fairly tough here in Australia, so we'd be better prepared for when things got really tough overseas. We concluded that folks called this missionary training section of the course 'Boot Camp' with good reason.

It was within days of our arrival at Plumpton that we received news that Betty's mother, Doris, had died of a heart attack. Our dear friends at Rochedale Baptist Church flew us back to Brisbane to attend her funeral. Their help during this very difficult time would be the first of many blessings we would receive from this awesome group of people.

Our first year in Western Sydney was taken up with studying the Bible and it was there that we were introduced to a chronological approach to studying the Scriptures by lecturer, Trevor McIlwain. Approaching the Bible as one unfolding, cohesive story from Genesis to Revelation really brought the book to life. This way of teaching gave us such a clear understanding of the nature and character of God and His gracious redemptive plan for His Creation which was fulfilled in the person and work of His Son, Jesus Christ. If we were ever to teach the Bible to those who had no access to it, we certainly wanted to present it in this way – a way that had made the Bible's true meaning become so clear in our own thinking.

On January 28, 1977, halfway through our two years of training at Plumpton, our twin daughters, Naomi and Anita, were born, six weeks premature. The day before their birth, Betty was admitted to hospital with what the doctors thought was an acute gallbladder infection. An x-ray was taken of her gallbladder and the discovery was made that Betty was having twins. The very next day they were born - just seven minutes apart. Upon arriving home with Anita, Betty was told by one of the single ladies, a fellow student, that she believed God would take us somewhere in the world where the people had some distorted superstitions about twins. Little did we know then that five years later her prediction would come true. But our faithful God would enable their little lives to have a lifesaving impact in changing that tragic aspect of the Tugutil's worldview.

God had his hand on the lives of our twins from the very

beginning. In her second week of life, Naomi inhaled some vomit, an emergency that disclosed a pre-existing *E.coli* lung infection that almost took her life. She remained in Blacktown hospital for another four long weeks while many people prayed that God would spare this new little life. None of us, at that time, knew of God's bigger plan for our identical twins in the lives of the Tugutil.

Our final year of training moved us to a place about thirty minutes outside Palmerston North in New Zealand. It was here that we would be taught how to learn an unwritten language while simultaneously acquiring an understanding of the people's culture. At least our student housing, while still very small, now had a kitchen sink and running water; the communal showers, toilets and laundry facilities were already a familiar way of life from our training days in Australia.

The bewildered look on the face of our lecturer - or possibly his gales of laughter when it was my turn to demonstrate my newly acquired language skills - greatly heightened my awareness of how incredibly hard I would need to work if I was to learn a new language, in fact two new languages. Our instructor felt that Betty, bless her heart, should pick up a new language fairly well, a fact that greatly irked me – with my highly competitive nature. No, deep down I was really so happy for her ... NOT!

So after three years of training it was home to Brisbane, thinking that within six months or so, we'd be off to Indonesia. But God and the Indonesian Government had other ideas about that timing and delayed the granting of our visas for almost two years. This gave a little extra time for our premature twins to build up their health and be that little bit older in preparation for the upcoming transition. Looking back now, we can also see that Betty and I were still young and fairly naive. A bit more maturity certainly didn't go astray before we began tackling the challenges that lay before us. That time also gave my parents and sisters a chance to have us living close by and they took every opportunity to enjoy our accessibility – my parents especially enjoying every moment with their much loved twin granddaughters. We were also able to spend time with Betty's dad who lived on the Sunshine Coast, about ninety minutes' drive north of Brisbane, and with her sister who lived in Brisbane. Adjusting to life in another country can involve a great personal cost for those who choose that lifestyle but the cost to their parents, grandparents and other loved ones can also be enormous.

Finally one evening the phone rang at home and it was our future co-workers, Don and Heather McCall, who were also waiting to head to Indonesia from their home in Perth. Don phoned with the news that our group of visas had come out of Immigration in Jakarta and we now had three months to be in the country. I was over the moon but Betty, now with three year old twins, was anticipating how difficult life could turn out to be in that strange county to our north. She was wary of the huge challenges that awaited us in this next chapter of our lives. In the late 70's, the internet, email and search engines like Google were still unheard of, so our means of obtaining accurate, current information was limited to the few books we could get our hands on. But Betty's convictions that Indonesia was where God wanted us and that every person should have the opportunity to accept or reject what God has done for them in Christ, were greater than her fears. And so our preparations for the move to this vast Southeast Asian country began in earnest.

- 2 -
INDONESIA, HERE WE COME

For I know the plans I have for you declares the Lord, plans for welfare and not for evil, to give you a future and a hope.

JEREMIAH 29:11

Our send off from the old Brisbane International Airport was amazing. Almost all of Rochedale church turned up to say goodbye, which was indicative of their commitment to faithfully partnering with us. Forever etched in our memories is a picture someone sent us of my mother perched halfway up a fence, a position that enabled her to get one final look at the family she knew she wouldn't see again for years.

On November 24, 1980, we flew to Perth, joined the McCalls and from there flew up to Jakarta. After spending three days in Jakarta and meeting the members of our Indonesian sponsoring board, it was on to Pontianak, the capital of Kalimantan Province on the island of Borneo. Pontianak was where we would spend the next year or so studying the Indonesian national language and culture.

In the lead-up to our departure from Australia, we had worked through the logistical problems of acquiring and moving things to Indonesia. Shipping arrangements required us to take the goods

THE TUGUTIL

to the Brisbane Wharf months before our actual departure. Other essential items that we still needed while in Australia - but also required in Indonesia - would be sent as unaccompanied baggage a day or two before we flew out. This was a much cheaper option than taking it with us as excess baggage. But the process of reclaiming our unaccompanied air freight at the Jakarta end would be fraught with difficulties, as we were soon to discover.

To assist that process, our man in Jakarta required my passport which he assured me would be returned in time for our departure to Pontianak where it would be required for reporting us in. Unfortunately that didn't happen and I couldn't help but notice the concerned expressions on the faces of our Jakarta Office Manager as we walked to board our plane to Pontianak.

Arriving at Supadio, Pontianak's airport, we were greeted by a large sign instructing all foreigners to report to the immigration officials with their passports and other travel documentation. I had very unwisely just read the book *Hostage in Jakarta* about an imprisoned missionary who almost died from diseases he contracted in prison and I could envisage in graphic detail myself without my passport also being detained and carted off to some bleak dungeon. It's amazing what situations like that do for your prayer life. The closer I got to that Immigration desk, the more intensely I prayed. Betty and I 'kindly' allowed the McCall family to precede us in the line; in fact I would have happily let the entire planeload of passengers line up in front of our family. Don and Heather eventually arrived at the desk and presented their passports and paperwork. It wasn't just the oppressive heat that had me sweating profusely as I attempted to put into words the explanation I hoped would avert my imminent arrest and incarceration. Here we were, just a few metres away from the stony-faced government official, lacking the little booklet that showed I had a valid visa permitting my entry into their country. Nervously waiting in line directly behind the McCalls, I heard the Immigration officer ask Don in English if we were travelling with them. I held my breath. The Immigration officer gestured to us that, since we were a party, we could all just proceed on through. Oh what a feeling of absolute overwhelming relief I experienced as we all walked on out of that airport terminal! God had certainly answered our prayers and would do so on many more occasions over the coming years.

The Pontianak Mission Guest House was very full when we arrived. Our adjustments were not just limited to daily life in Indonesia but also to living with the Americans who comprised the majority of our mission's personnel. Our first American breakfast next morning seemed so different to what was 'normal' in Australia. Guests all shared one bathroom and that room contained a toilet bowl, a large cement water container and a small bucket-like bowl with a handle used to scoop up the cold water and throw it over yourself. This was their substitute for a shower. It also acted as a source of water for flushing the toilet. Having only one of these bathrooms became a huge problem when another missionary and I both came down with the worst case of diarrhoea either of us had ever experienced. Unfortunately, we both frequently needed to use that room at the same time, to say nothing of the requirements of all the other guests. Being so sick and still quite convinced I'd eventually face dire consequences for not yet having my passport, I desperately wanted to get on the first plane back to Australia.

Unfortunately, our church had misunderstood our instructions for sending on their financial support and were therefore still awaiting our advice on how best to send it to us. There were insufficient funds in our account to purchase even one ticket home let alone tickets for the entire family. We were stuck there and so I had no choice but to endure my massive case of culture shock, like it or not. I will always remember the day when my long-awaited passport finally arrived and we were all officially reported in and registered with the appropriate authorities. The return of my passport removed one major source of my stress but, as we moved from the guest house to our rented house in suburban Pontianak, we would soon realise that more stress lay just around the corner.

- 3 -
LIVING IN PONTIANAK

As you sent me into the world, so I have sent them into the world.

JOHN 17:18

After several days in the guest house we were informed that we would be moving into what would become our home in Pontianak for the next year. Now this involved some good news and some bad news. It was good news that we were about to get settled into our own house and could begin our language and culture studies in earnest. The bad news was that we had no vehicle to transport ourselves around. But the other piece of good news was that a missionary on home leave in the United States was happy for our family to use their 100cc motorbike for the next few months until they returned.

Then came our next bit of bad news. Lynn Haines, the Pontianak supply man and office manager, took me to pick up the motorbike and then it was back to the guesthouse to get Betty and the girls so we could all go and see where we'd be living for the next year or so. Fortunately I had obtained a motorbike licence in Australia a few months prior to our arrival but I had never carried anyone else on the bike, as it's illegal to do so within the first year of getting an Australian licence. But that law certainly didn't apply in Indonesia.

Thinking that we would all go together in the mission's van, you can imagine my shock when Lynn told me that our entire family could all fit on the little 100cc motor bike and that 'everyone travels that way over here'. Eventually off we all rode with one of the girls perched on the tank, then me, then the other twin, and finally Betty side saddle (which was the culturally accepted way for a woman to sit on the bike as a passenger) on the remaining bit of seat. Dodging and weaving solo through the chaotic Pontianak traffic on the bike while trying to keep Lynn in my sights would have been stressful enough, but doing that with the family on board took me to the extreme limits of my coping ability. Thank God, somehow we managed to arrive safely at the house.

Then came more bad news. The missionary couple who had previously been living in the house had not been able to move out as planned. Therefore, we would initially be living there with them until they were able to get on a charter plane that allowed missionaries to fly free to Sulawesi whenever space was available. No one could tell us exactly how long that would take.

The bad news just kept on coming. The two bedroom house had one very large bedroom and one very small bedroom. The couple, who had no children at the time and expected to be leaving at any moment, were very well settled into the much larger bedroom that was also packed full of their gear still waiting to be shipped. That meant that the only place left for all four of us was in the other tiny little bedroom. Its furniture comprised a set of bunk beds and one small cupboard. Life for us would be very cosy until that free plane ride eventuated!

As we were processing all of this unwelcome information, bad news item four settled upon us. Our sleeping arrangements comprised Betty taking one twin in the lower bunk and me, the other twin on the top bunk. Our first night's sleep in the house was interrupted by what sounded like a herd of elephants running across the ceiling above us. The noise turned out to be several huge sewer rats scampering back and forth in the ceiling. Knowing it was all going on just above our heads - along with the oppressive heat and humidity - did nothing to help us nod off to a peaceful night's sleep.

Just when we thought there couldn't possibly be any more bad news, there was. Just before dawn we were awakened by the blaring sound of the call to prayer from the mosque just down the road. I think the idea must be to ensure the awakening of all good Muslims, giving them no chance of getting back to sleep, so they then get up and go off to the mosque to pray. Sadly though, the call doesn't just wake members of that particular faith. With the first almighty burst of sound emanating at a decibel level designed to ensure it achieved its desired outcome, we just about jumped out of bed wondering what in heaven's name was going on. Eventually though, one does become somewhat accustomed to the call and if not, ear plugs or having a music player with earphones by the bed can make the situation somewhat tolerable.

But if we thought that we were doing it tough, we just needed to give some thought to the situation that Don and Heather were in. Their first house in Pontianak was so riddled with termites that leaning hard up against a wall would certainly demolish it. Eventually they were moved into a better house built over the overflow of the city drainage system that could only be accessed by walking along an elevated board walk. Their biggest struggle, though, was with their two year old daughter Rebecca, who had started having severe asthma attacks. Deeply concerned for her health, they were able to procure an air conditioner for her room which led to a significant improvement in her condition.

Eventually our house mates, Steve and Mary, a wonderful couple who would also end up working in Maluku Province, did get their plane ride and we were left on our own, though not for long. We soon discovered that just living in Pontianak could be very time consuming and we were advised to employ an Indonesian 'pembantu' or house helper so that we could better utilise our time for study. Our language program coordinator dropped in and informed us that the only 'pembantus' still available were two girls in their late teens who had just come out from an interior tribe in order to go to senior high school.

The arrangement was that we would need to take both girls. It would be too lonely for one girl on her own, especially as this was their very first time living in a town, away from their tribe. We would give them a place to stay, feed and clothe them, cover all schooling costs and their transport back and forth to their home village as well as provide them with a small wage. In exchange they would cook meals, clean the house and give us someone to frequently converse with in the language.

Having these two girls living with us who knew almost no English would force us all to use our - at that stage - very limited Indonesian. Those early days were interesting as we tried our best to communicate with them and they with us. Within the first week, they handed us a letter written in Indonesian. It turned out to be a list of complaints and demands. We took that to an older missionary lady with the mission group who had assisted the girls in enrolling in high school. She negotiated a settlement that seemed reasonable to us and pleasing to the girls. Eventually our ability to communicate grew and we were very thankful for the blessing Suria and Nimuh were to us and our little girls.

Our mode of transport in Indonesia - the family motorbike with the four of us on it. Heather and Rebecca can be seen in the background

- 4 -
MORE TALES FROM PONTIANAK

Do not lay up for yourselves treasures on Earth, where moth and rust destroy and where thieves break in and steal.

MATTHEW 6:19

Gradually life settled into a pattern of language study. Slowly, all that had initially seemed so strange became less and less abnormal. One of those incredibly 'different' things to us was the large open drains or 'parits' that crisscross the city and carry the city's waste water and sewerage out to the sea with the tides. This, we eventually discovered, was what our toilet emptied into and it was unpleasant to even contemplate that fact when watching people washing themselves and cleaning their teeth in that water.

Another interesting aspect of our new life was the system that delivered the town's water supply. The facilities struggled to cope because of the city's rapid population growth. This meant that during the dry season little or no water flows from the tap over the 'bak' or large cement tub in the bathroom that stored all the water required for the home. Buying a pump and then tapping into the water pipe coming into the yard from the street gave the best chance of obtaining water which, incidentally, had to be well boiled or treated before drinking. During dry season, a pump would only work at night and sometimes only in the very early hours of the morning when demand was especially low. One night I set up the pump in the front yard and having no success finding water, returned to my study thinking I'd try again on the half hour. When I came out to check the pump, hunched over it was a man who must have thought he needed it far more than we did. I immediately screamed 'Pencuri, pencuri!', ('Thief, thief!') which sent him frantically running off, fearing the terrible beating he would have received from the neighbours had he been caught.

Now I was fully aware that an unguarded pump in my front yard was too much of a temptation for the city's thieves. I decided that the problem could be very simply overcome by purchasing a large, solid chain and a very hefty padlock. Once the pump was firmly secured to the incoming water pipe, there was no way anyone could get it unless they had the trusty key and I alone possessed that. That night I went to bed assured that I needn't bother to bring the pump inside the house. No one was going to get their thieving hands on that baby!

Unfortunately I slept right through that night, totally missing the alarm I'd set for one o'clock in the morning so that I could again check for water. Immediately I woke next morning and went to check the pump just in case, by some chance, there may have been some water available to pump. But that night my enterprising 'pencuri' friend had returned for another try. Seeing my efforts to thwart his desperate endeavours, he had surveyed the situation and decided that he could still take it by disconnecting the pipe where it came in from the road and then also half way down the side of our house. This would enable him to simply walk off with the lot. Gone was the pump, the lock and chain, meters of piping that the pump was chained to, along with our water meter.

This all cost a small fortune to replace and never again was the new pump used without my fervent and constant supervision.

We made it through that year, being robbed only two other occasions. Once I was pickpocketed on a bus and then, after packing up the house ready to move over to Maluku, we returned from our send-off party to find we'd been broken into and a number of things taken.

Despite a number of setbacks and discouragements, we managed to acquire enough Indonesian language for our field leaders to give us the okay to move into a tribal ministry. During our time in Pontianak, our twins, who were now four, had simply played daily with the neighbour kids and had acquired the Indonesian language at an unbelievable rate. Not only did they know what to say but their pronunciation and natural cadence had them sounding just like their little Indonesian friends. How Betty and I wished that our own eloquence in the language was so praiseworthy, but we both knew that was highly unlikely. It was to be - for some time yet - still well out of our reach.

It was in our last couple of months in Pontianak that Keith and Anita Miles visited us and asked if we would consider teaming up with their family and going to a province in eastern Indonesia where our organisation had not previously worked. This would mean that initially there would be no support services in place. These included guest houses, people who would constantly buy and ship our supplies to us, saving us the travel in and out of our tribal location, and government representatives, who do all the paperwork necessary to keep us in the country. Things could be pretty tough in the early days. The availability of hospitals and medical supplies were high priorities on Betty's list. In Pontianak, the girls had experienced bouts of sickness including malaria and migraine headaches, but there we had had access to a great little Baptist hospital several hours bus ride north.

Agreeing to move to an unknown situation was a huge step of faith for Betty. I think we both really wanted to be 'good' tribal missionaries and at that time we thought 'good' meant those missionaries who tackled the most difficult challenges. So up went our hands to head off with the Miles family to the relative unknowns of the Province of Maluku. Soon our friends, the McCalls, also agreed to join the team once they'd finished their Indonesian studies which they were completing while helping out in tribal work in West Kalimantan.

- 5 -
THE MOVE TO NORTH MALUKU

Be strong, and let your heart take courage, all you who wait for the Lord!

PSALM 31:24

Keith and Anita had now been living in Central Sulawesi for some time and Keith, along with Steve, the former occupant of our Pontianak house, had visited Maluku to determine the likelihood of our organisation working in that province. Four animistic tribal groups were identified that had never been exposed to the Gospel. Keith felt particularly drawn to the Tugutil people while Steve was keen to enter one of the other locations on the island of Taliabu. Steve would initially base out of Ambon in the south but that was too far from Halmahera where the Tugutil were living. So Keith and Anita, along with their two youngest children, Eric and Kevin, found a large, old house in Tobelo that could accommodate our two families. This way we could share the outlay for the rent, which was required to be paid upfront for the entire length of the lease. The rental term is commonly two or three years, and sometimes much longer. Tobelo is a small coastal town with a natural harbour from which we would do a more detailed survey to determine the most suitable location to begin working with the people.

THE TUGUTIL

In 1982, the town had just opened its first bank, had one frequently 'out of order' telephone - for the entire town - at the post office, and had no electricity, running water or toilet paper.

Surrounded by mountains, this little town was stiflingly hot and humid, unless an easterly breeze came in off the ocean. It did however have an old ex-Japanese all-weather airstrip a couple of hours drive to the north, just beyond another even smaller village known as Galela. After hearing about this airstrip, our mission pilot based in Pontianak offered to fly us there with all our gear in the mission's six seater Cessna 185. He figured it would take two trips but the journey wouldn't cost us much more than flying commercially. It would certainly be a lot less hassle for us and he could then take a look at the province where, he hoped one day to set up a flight program. With all the boat travel we had ahead of us, we had no idea at the time how we would long for that day to come.

Our first few days in the Tobelo house certainly attracted the attention of hordes of people, including many young children. Having two cute, white, four-year-old twin girls was such a novelty that word quickly spread and soon every available window and door was crammed packed with people's heads straining to get a look. Naomi and Anita, seeing a multitude of young children, seized the opportunity to do what they had done so often with the kids in our street in Pontianak. They quickly proceeded to organise all the kids in the front yard to play school. This time they would get to play teacher and all the children would be their pupils. So in their perfect Indonesian, and to roars of laughter from all the adult onlookers, they assembled the children and proceeded to teach exactly as their little Pontianak friends had often done with them. This broke down barriers and gave us a great introduction into the Tobelo community. Whenever we walked downtown it would be to the constant call of 'Helo Nomi dan Nita, mari, sini dulu!' ('Hello Naomi and Anita, come and visit me!') Naomi and Anita would be involved in the bridal parties of two weddings and were much loved by many in the town.

Our time in Tobelo gave us lots of contact with a small Baptist church and a tiny Bible College attached to the church. It was members of this church who were instrumental in inviting our organisation to work among the Tugutil. Pastor and Mrs Layang, originally from the southern Philippines, headed up the Baptist work and did all they could to help us settle into the community and prepare us for the move over to Lili. They organised several members of one of their congregations to accompany us on survey trips and to undertake the chain sawing of lumber for the building of our houses. They also built the other major item required if we were to reach the Tugutil, a boat big enough to carry loads in the vicinity of a ton but not so big that five or six people couldn't haul it up onto the beach when not in use. I suppose it was similar in size to those used by surf lifesaving clubs in Australia - only with the addition of a cabin to provide protection from the weather.

One of the saddest memories of our months living in Tobelo occurred the day after our arrival in the town. Keith had been alerted to the plight of a family from a very poor Baptist congregation located up near the airstrip. Apparently, a mother had sent one of her young children to purchase kerosene for a lamp but the trader had instead accidentally provided petrol. Upon the child's return with the lamp still alight, the young mother attempted to top up its supply of fuel only to have it explode in her hands. This resulted in horrific burns to much of her torso and neck. Years before we arrived, Canadian Mennonite missionary doctors had established a small but very effectively run hospital in the town. However, due to the increasing numbers of doctors being trained in Indonesia, the Government deemed the Mennonites' presence as no longer necessary and withdrew their visas. The hospital continued to operate but the standard of care plummeted and much of its equipment went missing. Keith, aware that Betty was a nurse, took her to see the woman, who was in an appalling state and experiencing incredible pain.

Writing about the experience, Betty recorded the following:

> 'This so called "hospital" has been responsible for my biggest culture shock since arriving here - it defies description. Despite having some nursing staff available, the husband - a simple farmer - has to change his wife's dressings for her extensive third degree burns every second day. He knows very little about basic hygiene but is doing the best he knows how. The burns are badly infected and I am doing my best to make her as comfortable as possible. Since bringing her here to Tobelo, wild pigs have completely destroyed their gardens so when the family does return home, they will have little to eat. The husband and five young children are all accommodated on the floor of her hospital room, which is in an old tuberculosis ward that has goats and chickens wandering in and out.
>
> In the first week of visiting her daily, she asked if I would bring some scissors to cut her hair as she was finding the head lice really difficult to cope with. The next day as I cut her hair I found both of her ears were charcoal. This had gone unnoticed, as the hair had covered her ears. After another month of extreme suffering this dear lady passed away, a death that may not have occurred had she been able to receive care in a modern, well equipped hospital.'

The harbour and town of Tobelo in 2006

Naomi and Anita playing with the neighbourhood children

- 6 -
THE SURVEY TRIP

And behold, I am with you always, to the end of the age.

MATTHEW 28:20B

Although aware that the Tugutil people populated several distinct areas on Halmahera Island, we were still unsure exactly where they existed in their greatest numbers and which location would prove the best for working with them. We also required written permission from all relevant government departments. This necessitated a trip to a little town called Buli - the seat of local government. Previously Keith and I had met with the Bupati in Ternate. This gentleman, whose position in the government is one level under the provincial governor, gave us a warm and very profitable meeting. At the close of our time, the Bupati took us out into his waiting room that was filled with 'Camats', the guys who head up the tier of government immediately below and who were all waiting for their turn to meet with him. He introduced Keith and I and instructed them to give us their full co-operation. One of these men was the official to whom we would be required to report in Buli, along with the local police.

Pastor Layang, the Baptist minister from Tobelo, a very

THE TUGUTIL

experienced seaman, along with his teenage nephew, Yafet, agreed to take us to Buli in our new wooden boat. Before moving into our tribal location we would make this journey several times. These trips would allow us to gather information that would help us to determine the most strategically advantageous spot in which to locate ourselves among the tribal people. Walking down to the boat on one such trip, Keith commented to me that he knew people in the States who would pay a fortune to go on an adventurous trip like the one we were about to embark upon. That made me feel really privileged until I considered the fact that we were outlaying a small fortune by the time we had paid for the boat, motors, food and hundreds of litres of fuel for the 450 kilometres round trip.

So off we went on a journey that we thought may take up to three weeks, leaving Anita Miles, Betty and the girls at the house in Tobelo. Eric and Kevin Miles wanted to be in on the 'adventure', so they also joined us. Our plan was to sail directly to Buli making just one stop at a lumber camp. There we were given some bad deer meat resulting in very upset stomachs. This, along with a bad case of sunburn for Keith and me, had us feeling rather sorry for ourselves, but soon we were again on our way. Arriving in Buli we reported in and then, on our return trip, called in at different coastal villages to inquire about the tribal people. We did go to one village where a number of Tugutil had migrated and had 'masuk agama' or entered religion. Our permission to work with the people had been granted on the basis that they had not ever registered under one of the five recognised religions permitted by the Government, something prohibited under Indonesian law. After the attempted communist coup that brought President Suharto to power, this law was introduced as an anti-communist measure requiring all Indonesians to belong to one of the five recognised religions at that time. These Tugutil people, who were now considered as having already 'entered religion', were off limits to us as were members of the Islamic faith. Next it was on to a lumber company camp situated on the coast, from where, at that time, large logs were being shipped out to Japan. During our stay we were told how their company's survey crews would only go into Tugutil territory if accompanied by an armed military escort due to their fear of the tribal people.

The next morning a strong southerly had begun blowing a gale, just as we were due to continue our trip. This would make travel on the ocean in our small boat far too dangerous and so it was decided that we should delay travelling until the wind calmed down. After two more days of waiting and feeling like we could wait no longer, we decided to set off at first light, hopefully before the wind became too strong. It wasn't long after leaving the camp that we needed to change our easterly course and follow the coast northwards. With huge waves now pounding the boat sending seawater pouring in, we needed to alter our course immediately. But changing course would necessitate turning side on to these monster waves – a manoeuvre that could very easily capsize us. The only option was to keep heading east and moving further and further out to sea.

The farther we travelled from shore, the more concerned I became about our safety. Once again some desperate prayers went up but nothing seemed to change the ferocity of the wind and the size of the waves. Then it struck me that this may actually be the end of us. Many boats sink in those waters and I was seriously beginning to think that we might be next in line to meet that end. Again my praying became more intense and I must admit that with nothing changing, the doubts began to assail my thinking.

What if God didn't actually answer prayer? In fact, what if the atheists were correct after all and I'd been sucked into believing a lie? The doubts only lasted a minute or so as I began to recall the numerous times God had amazingly answered prayer for us in times of dire need. But the ferocious waves just kept hammering our little boat which made me truly believe that our end was nigh. Now my prayers were for my family. I found myself acknowledging that although I couldn't understand why God would allow us to drown when we hadn't even seen the Tugutil, He is God and ultimately has every right to call the shots… and I needed to let Him.

It seemed that once I acknowledged His right to be God and have His way, whatever that might look like, a small break of calm appeared between two huge waves. Immediately Nelson Layang spun the boat around and the next thing we knew, our boat was travelling with the waves rather than against them. The boat went surfing down a huge wave headed back in a north-westerly direction towards the shore. Soon we were able to land the boat at a small village called Sosolat. I can't begin to describe my relief at still being alive when my trembling feet once again felt solid ground beneath them.

After landing, we were met by some people who took us to the head man of the village. He was keen to know who we were and what we were up to. Once informed of our quest to find the Tugutil, and seeing our letters of permission from the Government, he told us about a group of Tugutil who were camped just a couple of kilometres further north and offered to take us up to them and translate for us. After a relatively short walk, we entered a small plot of cleared ground where there were several small shelters and about a dozen or so tribal people. Through our translator we were able to gather information and found that this group would move up and down the coast staying in one location for several months and then moving on.

Keith Miles, with camera in hand, requested that our translator ask the people for permission to take photos. Many years later, we would discover that in actual fact he had instead simply ordered them to line up with their weapons so that Keith could photograph them. We would also discover that this enraged one young man, Habiana, who was so angry that he decided not just to pose with his bow and arrow but also demonstrate how he could kill with it. Many years later, he told us that he drew back his bow string and aimed his arrow at Pastor Layang, intending to kill him. However, as he went to discharge the arrow he found it impossible to release until all tension was taken off the bow string. That morning God had saved our lives in the boat and a couple of hours later He saved Nelson Layang from being shot by Habiana's arrow. I have no doubts that our mission leaders would have immediately pulled the plug on us working with the Tugutil had Habiana succeeded.

After our first encounter with the tribal people, we moved further north to the village of Dorasago and it was there that we heard of an area alongside the Lili River where a number of Tugutil families were settled. The village head man took us on the long hike down the coast to meet the people and they seemed to have no objection to us moving in to live with them alongside the Lili River. Eventually, we did get back to Tobelo feeling that Lili would be a choice location to live and work among these mysterious people. After arriving back, and remembering his comment about his friends in the States who would willingly pay a fortune to go on our 'adventure', Keith told me that as far as he was concerned he'd had just about enough adventure to last him a lifetime. They were my sentiments exactly.

These pictures were taken at the time of
our first contact with the Tugutil

- 7 -
MAYBE THOSE STORIES WERE TRUE

> Nebuchadnezzar answered, 'Blessed be the God of Shadrach, Meshach, and Abednego, who has sent his angel and delivered his servants, who trusted in him...'
>
> DANIEL 3:28

Although we were totally unaware of it at the time, and ever so thankful for that ignorance, there was a second attempt to murder one of our team in those early days. A young man, Muru, came asking for medication for a really bad headache. This occurred on one of our initial trips into the area for the purpose of building temporary housing. As a team we had decided right from the beginning of the work that we would implement a strategy to see the medical program indigenised as soon as possible. Therefore, in preparation for it to eventually become self-sustaining, we would need to introduce the concept of exchanging something for the medicines they received. In the event that we had to leave, we hoped to have trained them to be able to continue to provide some very basic level of health care for their own people as nothing was available locally.

The Tugutil had no money to cover even a portion of the cost of medication nor, at that time, did they understand the concept of money. Medicine would initially need to be given in exchange for a small amount of food. We would fully cover the cost of all medicines and then gradually, as the cash crop component of our community development projects began to bear fruit, progressively reduce the amount of the subsidy. Bananas were one kind of food in plentiful supply in Lili at the time and so guess what we got almost every time someone needed medicine, soap or matches. It was not uncommon for us to have six or seven full stalks of bananas hanging from the rafters at the back of our house. Betty would serve us up fresh bananas, dried bananas, fried bananas, banana soup, banana cake and banana milkshakes. Any bananas left - after our visitors had helped themselves to copious amounts - were then given to our chickens and our dog, who also grew to love them.

Now back to the story of Muru. The tribal culture demanded the immediate handover of anything requested. Of course, this system had all kinds of strings attached and soon the giver would expect to have his turn on the receiving end. So Muru resisted bringing even a couple of bananas to exchange for the medicine and grew increasingly angry with Keith's insistence that some exchange first take place. Finally, after staring at Keith for hours with a look that could kill, he eventually gave in and agreed to go home and get some small item of food to give for the pain killers to relieve his headache.

As Muru began the thirty-minute journey inland towards his house, Keith noticed him taking an unfamiliar trail. Keith thought little of it, figuring that Muru might just be avoiding the need to cross the Lili River. The only trail heading inland that we knew about crossed the river twice. We were nervous that a time would come when we would be in the interior region visiting people and the river would flood, preventing us from returning home. Keith quickly called the young man who was interpreting for us, getting him to ask Muru if it would be okay for him to tag along so we could also learn of this alternative trail that he hoped would eliminate the need for a river crossing. In those early days, we were unaware of Muru's fearsome reputation as a bad-tempered man, someone to be avoided when angry. His fiery temper made him volatile and dangerous. Of all the people to upset, Keith had unknowingly picked one of the worst. About twenty minutes into the trip, Muru, carrying his razor sharp machete, hung back on purpose to position Keith in front of him on the trail. When Keith finally realised the perilous position he had now placed himself in, once again, desperate prayers went up for protection. They reached a place where two large trees had fallen across the trail. It was necessary to climb up onto the first tree trunk, follow it for a bit and then jump down and walk along the other, to re-join the trail. Muru, who had been furious with Keith all morning, apparently decided this would be an ideal spot on which to remove Keith's head. When Keith jumped down onto the second tree trunk, his head was at the perfect height to be severed by one good swing of Muru's razor-sharp machete. Muru was poised directly above Keith. As he went to raise his weapon to deliver the fatal blow, he found himself unable to lift it above waist height.

Incredibly, Muru became a Christian and many years later he told this story at a Bible study. Keith was in attendance at the time and heard, for the first time, about Muru's attempt to decapitate him and God's miraculous intervention. Muru, today a totally transformed man, described what happened as he tried to raise his machete to deliver the fatal blow. It was as if someone's arms were wrapped tightly around his arms, restraining him from lifting the machete above his waist. This frightened Muru and on the spot he decided that we must have stronger 'medicine' or powers than he did, so he quickly dropped any plan to kill Keith out of a great fear that these powers would seek retribution. There is no doubt that God was protecting us during those turbulent days knowing that one day we would present His good news and see an amazing response among these people.

Tugutil 'currency' – bananas

Muru being restrained by a number of
men during one of his outbursts

- 8 -
UNDER ATTACK

The Lord is my light and my salvation— whom shall I fear?
The Lord is the stronghold of my life; of whom shall I be afraid?

PSALM 27:1

Numerous delays hindered our move into the tribe but at 2.30 am on October 25th 1982, we were finally on our way. We had discovered that a small copra boat was returning empty to a village near Lili, so arrangements were made to load our gear onto the boat and accompany it. Our family headed down to the Tobelo dock and we headed off on the twelve-hour ocean trip to Lili. This very first boat trip to Lili as a family was blessed with amazingly calm seas and there were no mishaps for the entire trip.

After arriving and settling into a small, seven by three metre dwelling that a team of us had erected on a previous visit, it would be only a few weeks until the Miles family headed off to begin their journey back to the US for eleven months of home leave. Back then, it was usual practice for our personnel to spend almost a year back in their passport country after completing five years in the field.

Immediately after our first furlough, the five year term was reduced to four. The Miles' departure left our family alone with

THE TUGUTIL

the Tugutil but, except for a few occasions, we felt quite safe living there among them. Surely that could only have been the peace of God guarding our hearts despite the many uncertainties surrounding us. However, despite feeling safe, life in Lili did feel very isolated. We were cut off from all forms of contact with the outside world. With our SSB radio permission still not granted, communication with other mission personnel was not possible although had an emergency occurred, I would not have hesitated setting it up and using it.

Even though we had virtually zero knowledge of the language, we had learnt about a dozen or so language acquisition phrases. This allowed us to rock up to someone's house and say such things as, 'Hello friend, how are you?' We practised these phrases over and over until they sounded quite natural and fluent. Ironically, because of our convincing introductions, when we met people for the first time they immediately assumed we could speak their language and promptly launched into a barrage of words that made absolutely no sense to us. After finishing their monologue and probably noticing blank and bewildered expressions on our faces, it was then our turn to roll out some more well-rehearsed phrases.

Most commonly, this follow-up message was employed: 'I didn't understand anything you just said. I only know a tiny little bit of your language but I do want to learn more. Can you help me do that?' Then would come their next response. Again, none of it made any of sense to us.

Visiting the people in their houses usually involved asking if we could sit down. After this pleasantry, we would roll out the questions.

'What is this? What is that?' and we would frantically try to write down their responses phonetically. As the tribal people possessed very few household items, the process was completed quickly. After covering everything in sight, much to my relief and I imagine theirs as well, I would roll out my final parting phrase.

'I'm going home,' and off I would go. It was so good when Betty and the girls accompanied me on these visits as their presence was a brilliant distraction after I had exhausted my very limited vocabulary.

Another important task involved mapping the area and doing a census. This required recording each family member's name and the location of their house in the area. Two things greatly complicated this process. Firstly, it was taboo for a person to use the name of their in-law. This meant that each person could be referred to by more than one name, depending on their family relationships. All of this was very confusing if you didn't know about the taboo, as was the case with me. Also the semi-nomadic lifestyle of the tribal people could, within months, render our maps indicating their place of abode totally useless.

On one of those days when I'd been attempting to do some mapping and using my very limited language, I returned home to prepare the kerosene pressure lamps that would light up our tiny cabin after dark. Betty had spent the day with the girls doing school work and trying her best with her very limited language to communicate with the people who came wanting our help with various things. Some, of course, came to simply stand and stare at these strange, long nosed, white people and silently observe our household activities, probably quite mysterious to them.

One day we had a visit from a tribal lady who lived way up in the interior of the island and seldom came out to the coast. Betty had just opened a large can of powdered milk and had laid the shiny lid down on the table. The woman, attracted by the lid, picked it up and, seeing her reflection, leapt backwards in shock. It was probably the first time she had ever seen her own reflection with such clarity.

I take my hat off to the amazing ladies who willingly put themselves in these situations for the sake of the Gospel. They are true superheroes and I very much include Betty, Heather, Anita and Otari in that category. The constant heat and humidity meant that by early evening we were all exhausted. Generally, after taking a bath in the river, we would eat whatever Betty was able to manage to get together for dinner, have a Bible story for the girls and then all be off to bed in our one bedroom, hopefully temporary, accommodation.

One night, after settling into bed, we were just drifting off to sleep when a sudden, loud racket interrupted the usual night-time jungle noises. It came from our iron roof. It sounded like a barrage of rocks was hailing down on our little jungle cabin. My thoughts immediately leapt to stories about the lumber company survey teams who refused to enter the area for fear of being attacked at night by the tribal people. Was this an attempt to drive us out of the area? If so, it sure was effective – because we were scared witless. But, moments later, we heard a voice call in perfect New Zealand-accented English, 'Anybody home?'

It was Don McCall and our mission pilot Scott Wolf who had arrived to scout out possible airstrip locations. Without radio contact, we'd had no idea they were coming. As they were crossing the river just below our house, they decided that they would have some fun with us. So each grabbed a handful of gravel from the river bed. If it hadn't been so good to see familiar faces and hear English spoken again, I think we may have left them outside all night to fight off the malaria carrying mosquitoes as payback.

Once apologies had been given and … kind of received, the visitors were fed and we all turned in for the night. Unfortunately, the only spot available for them to sleep was in the other small room in our cabin, between sacks of rice and flour. But that room was not as well sealed off from the larger jungle critters as was our bedroom. In the morning we awoke to hear Don and Scott complaining that they had slept terribly. An invading force of bush rats - seeking to get into our bags of flour and rice - had crawled all over them throughout the night. Maybe we should have felt a bit more sympathy for them both, but after the scare they had given us with their 'rocks on the roof' stunt, well… that certainly wasn't going to happen.

Our first jungle house was a 7 X 3 metre shed that eventually had a second storey extension added on

- 9 -
THE SINKING

To you, O Lord, I cry, and to the Lord I plead for mercy.

PSALM 30:8

In September, 1982, about a month before our family had moved into the tribe, Don and Heather McCall, with their young daughters Rebecca and Esther, arrived in Tobelo. The plan was for us all to move to Lili together but they were unable to get the necessary government approval that would allow them to make the move together with us. Miles had left for eleven months home assignment in America and Chris Lahu, a graduate of a Baptist theological college in Manado and our newest Indonesian team member, was busy in town getting married to a lovely young lady, Otari. She had worked for Australian missionaries in Sulawesi, and had also attended the same theological college as Chris. This very special Indonesian couple would bring amazing gifts and abilities to our team, something for which we were ever so thankful. This turn of events left us as the only members of our team on location in the tribe. It was decided that our little boat should remain out in Tobelo enabling the McCalls to come in as soon as they received government permission to move. Their plan was to join us in Lili before Christmas, 1982.

In early December however, I came down with malaria, quickly followed by the rest of the family. Sadly, in the rush to get packed and moved in, we had neglected to pack our mosquito nets. This was a serious issue, as all the boards used to wall up our little house had been nailed up immediately after being chain sawed, and after weeks of exposure to the hot sun, had dried out and significantly shrunk. This left gaps between each board that allowed malaria-laden mosquitoes to enter our tiny house and feed on us as we slept.

Meanwhile, back in town, Don and Heather had been informed that their paperwork had still not come through and so they would not be able to join us until some time in the New Year. With no radio contact to tell us of the delay, Don decided to make a trip into Lili in our little one ton boat to update us and bring in the supplies we had ordered in advance to accompany them had they been able to join us. When Don arrived he discovered four very sick people all down with malaria and so the decision was made to take us all out to town where there were two Indonesian doctors. Shortly after arriving, Betty and Naomi suffered particularly bad relapses that had me extremely concerned for them both. It is in times of serious sickness that you long to be near quality medical facilities, yet the reality is that so many people in this world lack even the very basics. This was certainly the case for the Tugutil.

Staying in the little town of Tobelo meant that we could enjoy a few niceties of life that were not available in the jungle. I say 'a few' because, at that time, this little town with a population of around six thousand still lacked much of what we would consider basic services - including electricity and town water. It had one paved road, a few dozen motor bikes, trucks and minivans.

THE SINKING

Once recovered from malaria, our family was able to take a wonderful week's break in Ternate staying with a lovely American missionary family, Doug and Phyllis Copp, who worked with a Pentecostal mission. Ternate is the commercial capital of North Maluku, so it had seen much more development than Tobelo. Most major items were available in the stores in Ternate, including a particular brand of toilet paper for which we were extremely thankful. As Tobelo stores did not yet carry what for us was a fairly essential item, we were always returning from Ternate with at least a one hundred roll carton in tow.

With our Ternate break and Christmas behind us, our attention now turned to returning to the tribe. However, in the meantime the weather had taken a turn for the worse with strong winds whipping up the ocean – creating a very dangerous situation for boat travel.

Finally the McCalls' paperwork arrived and they were now free to move into Lili. Each morning we would wake and immediately look to the sky. We'd see the clouds flying by, a good indicator that the wind was still fairly strong. We would listen out for the sound of the wind which, at that time, was blowing a gale. As a final check, we'd walk down to the beach and survey the condition of the ocean, hoping there'd be no white caps. But daily we would return home, yet again terribly disappointed. Days became weeks and weeks dragged into months but the howling winds refused to let up.

On the last day of February, the ocean conditions still hadn't seen any real improvement. But that day news arrived of an 80 ton copra boat that would be going right past Lili on its way to Buli, a small town about 95 kilometres further on around the coast. We decided that, despite the rough seas, we could not miss this opportunity to get back to the tribe. The large boat would allow us to take all the McCalls' moving in supplies, the drums of fuel required for our boat and a 240-volt generator. This would at least give us several hours of electricity each evening. Arrangements were quickly made with the boat captain and packing up began in earnest. That night, with all the supplies loaded, I took our family, Heather and their girls along with Chris' new wife Otari, on board the large boat, while Don and Chris loaded sufficient fuel on our little boat to get to Lili, a 130 km journey across open ocean.

We set out together from Tobelo at around 10 pm, and it wasn't long before we hit a violent storm that began throwing our big boat around and making most of us terribly sea sick. Again I have to say how much admiration I have for Betty and the girls, who spent so much of their time on boats suffering terrible seasickness. That hardship was seen by them as simply a price to be paid in order to reach the people. That trip would rank among the worst we would ever experience while travelling on boats in Indonesia.

Before heading out to sea, we had decided that Don and Chris would follow along behind us in our little boat. I would keep an eye out for them watching for a light that Don had set up so I could identify them in the dark. But in the wild storm we were quickly separated, and such was its ferocity that I soon became very concerned for their safety. Fearing that the little boat may have capsized, in desperation I approached our boat captain, asking him to turn back and look for Don and Chris. His response was to sternly inform me that to turn the boat side on to the huge waves would probably capsize us and there was nothing he could or would do to help.

Besides passing around a bucket for Betty, Naomi, Anita and Otari to fill due to their seasickness, most of that night I spent in

THE SINKING

prayer and trying to work out what I needed to do in the event that the guys had in fact drowned. In my mind I began formulating a plan to get Heather and their two little girls back to Australia and Chris' new wife, just married and now already a widow, back home to her family in Sulawesi. To my knowledge, in 1983 there was no such thing as a search and rescue service in that part of the country but I would need to report them to the police as missing. What would become of the Tugutil work? Obviously now, in light of what we were experiencing, I had begun preparing for the very worst.

Finally, as the sun rose on March 1st 1983, I heard the sound of outboard motors coming alongside our big boat. What a relief to see Don and Chris in that little boat! They had experienced a horrendous night on the ocean being tossed around in the wild seas and had in fact passed by us in the bigger boat without even sighting us. We were almost at Lili when Don pulled alongside our boat and suggested that we all come aboard in order to get the women and children ashore before commencing to unload the two tons of supplies and the fuel drums we had shipped in.

After boarding our little boat, it quickly became obvious that during the night it had taken on a lot of water, not good in these very rough conditions. Soon we were about 20 metres out from the place on shore where the families could disembark. Don began reversing the stern of the boat towards the shore allowing the front of the boat to ride the incoming waves. I had moved to the boat's bow and had thrown out the anchor and Don jumped into the waist deep water and began assisting Rebecca and Anita to get ashore. Just then a massive wave crashed over the boat. Within seconds, another huge wave smashed the boat's windscreen and swept Betty and Naomi out of the back of the boat slamming

Betty directly into one of the outboard motors. With Heather and their eighteen month old daughter Esther still inside the now submerged cabin, Don handed Anita to one of the onlookers standing near the water's edge and quickly started back to get to Heather and Esther. By then, another of the men on the beach had already reached the now mostly submerged boat and was helping extricate Heather and Esther. Don then took Esther and soon Heather and Esther joined the others who were all safely ashore. With the top of the cabin door totally under water, the only way out of the flooded boat was for Heather, tightly clutching Esther, to exit through the submerged door. Meanwhile Otari had managed to swim to the beach and Lus, a young teenager who had accompanied us to Lili, assisted Naomi make it ashore along with her much bruised mother. I re-entered the cabin and released Mile's dog who was tethered by a leash and frantically straining to keep her head above the water line. We were so thankful for the onlookers who rushed to our assistance. Soon we had everyone safely on shore, all sopping wet and Betty feeling bruised and battered from her encounter with the outboard motor.

Almost everything that we had taken with us on our little boat was now either lost or ruined from having been submerged in the ocean. Despite this, we were all so thankful to have survived that terrible night and the following morning's disaster that could have so easily ended in tragedy. Now, with our little boat sitting near the edge of the shore fully submerged, we wondered how we would unload our precious supplies from the large boat anchored off shore. Would the captain even wait for us to return?

Loaded on the deck of the boat that had now moved to a sheltered spot a few kilometres up the northern end of the Lili bay were more than two tons of building supplies and other gear, as well as several drums of fuel that needed to be quickly unloaded. Parked up on the beach were three small canoes and several men who were very willing to paddle me out to the boat to inform the boat captain of these latest developments. Within fifteen minutes I was climbing up onto the deck and heading to the wheelhouse to speak to the captain, who remained totally unaware of our plight.

Meanwhile, Don and Chris - with the help of many onlookers - set about recovering our doomed boat from the ocean floor. They retrieved the outboard motors and moved them up onto the shore. Don immediately got to work on the motors but we knew it would be some time before he would have them back in working order. Knowing we would need at least a full day before we could possibly have our boat and motor operational again, I asked the boat Captain if he would continue on to his final destination, load his cargo of copra and then call back in on the return trip for us to unload our supplies. His answer was an emphatic 'No.' He told me that we had just two hours to unload and anything left on board after that time had elapsed would be tossed overboard. My pleas fell on deaf ears and so, rather than waste precious time, we quickly loaded the small canoe and began shuttling the first load of supplies back to the beach. However, the place where our boat had sunk was far away from the sheltered spot where the cargo vessel was now anchored. It was far too rough to be able to successfully land the supplies at their intended destination. We realised that to get them unloaded quickly and safely, we would need to land them in the sheltered waters as close to the cargo vessel as possible .

After enlisting the other two canoes, we paddled back to the boat and began the huge task of ferrying the supplies ashore. Unfortunately, this was a long walk away from the beach shack we had built as a secure place to store fuel, outboard motors and the other supplies intended for our houses further inland. Incredibly, after many canoe trips over several hours, all that remained on the boat were our 200 litre drums of fuel. These we rolled into the ocean, swimming them to shore over a distance of about 300 metres. I clearly remember warily scanning the surface of the water for shark fins the whole time. I'm not real sure what I would have done had I actually spotted one except to kick harder but either the sharks weren't hungry that day or they were off hunting somewhere else and missed the easiest meal of their lives.

By late afternoon, we had ferried all the supplies and fuel ashore. Soon Don arrived. He came prepared to spend the night with the gear to ensure that nothing went missing. While we had been unloading the boat, Don had escorted the women and children to our house about 40 minutes' walk into the jungle. After seeing the families get reasonably settled, he and a couple of carpenters who had been working on extending our house walked back out to the coast, and then along the beach to the place where the supplies were now sitting. The carpenters, seeing that everything had already been unloaded, gathered up a few items that we had brought in for them and accompanied me on the walk back to our house. Don meanwhile, settled in for a night on the beach, watching over all our gear as a kind of beach security guard.

By the time we arrived at the place where the trail leaves the beach and entered the jungle, it was almost dark. Having absolutely no light source between the three of us, within just a few minutes we were facing pitch black darkness. Because the Tugutil always walked through the jungle in single file, the tracks were usually no more than about 40cm wide. In 1983 the jungle was still in its virgin state and the canopy of foliage above was incredibly dense, restricting the amount of light that could reach the ground below, even in daylight. By now, darkness had fallen and although there was a full moon, dense black storm clouds eliminated any vestige of available light. Being raised in the city, I must admit that being out in the jungle at night without a torch wasn't exactly something that filled my heart with joy. However, I certainly didn't want the Indonesians guys with me to see any indication of the fear I was experiencing. The thought of wandering off the track and getting lost in the vastness of the jungle didn't impress me one bit. I was fully aware that out in that jungle lived animals that could bite and that some of those bites involved poisons of various kinds. Although the island has no poisonous snakes, it is home to a large, toxic species of centipede, scorpions and many sizable pythons. At times, navigating the trail in the dark became impossible and the only method of ensuring that we were still on track was to get down on all fours and feel for the path. My ever-fertile imagination produced thoughts of placing my hand on a creature that was capable of giving me a very painful bite. This situation greatly motivated my prayer life as we progressed ever so slowly and carefully towards our simple jungle home, which was feeling more inviting than ever.

After what must have been close to an hour, we began to hear the sound of the river at the first of the two river crossings that were part of the journey home. As we exited the trees onto the sandy river bank, a break appeared in the cloud cover allowing the moonlight to stream down, illuminating the river. On the bank we could now see the glow of the fires from the tribal people's houses. Instantly I was overcome with an unspeakable sense of relief. To emerge from complete darkness into that wonderful light, filled me with an overwhelming sense of gratitude and joy. At that moment it was as though God reminded me of the darkness that bound the lives of the Tugutil and how wonderful and liberating it would be for them to come into His glorious light. That challenge remained with me during the many discouragements and hardships of the years that were to follow.

- 10 -
FIRE ON OUR BOAT

> Fear not, for I am with you; be not dismayed, for I am your
> God; I will strengthen you, I will help you, I will uphold you
> with my righteous right hand.
>
> ISAIAH 41:10

Having someone like Don on our team with his love of boats and expertise was such a blessing. Prior to his and Heather's arrival, our team was totally dependent on the locals for the building, maintaining and running of the little wooden boat that would become our means of transport in and out of Lili. Our dear friends from the Baptist church in Tobelo had a strong desire to see the Gospel go to the Tugutil and, although feeling that it was beyond their abilities, were keen to help enable us to make it happen. Unfortunately, their common sense did not always prevail when it came to advising us. It could be sometimes overridden, even at the expense of boating safety, by a desire to please us. We were to find out that any way to avoid saying a direct 'no' was an important part of their culture.

On one occasion this unfortunate state of affairs led to us grossly overloading our boat in an effort to get all of our building supplies into Lili in just one trip. In our minds, a single journey would save time and more importantly... money. I remember one passer-by commenting before our departure that the amount of freeboard on our overladen boat might be okay in sheltered waters but if we were going outside the protection of the Tobelo harbour, we could soon be taking on lots of water and end up in all kinds of trouble. That comment should have immediately set all kinds of alarm bells ringing… but no; we just merrily continued loading even more supplies on board. In recalling that occasion, what was really crazy was our intention to make a stop several hours down the coast and add more weight including three house builders along with all their accompanying gear. We surely could have starred in our own version of the movie, *Dumb and Dumber*.

Once we were fully loaded, or more correctly, overloaded, we set out on the ocean and it wasn't long before we were frantically bailing in order to remain afloat. The forward movement of our little boat helped a little, but the moment we stopped to load the three guys and their gear, we immediately began taking on water with every wave that hit the boat. The builders, seeing our perilous predicament, immediately swam out to the boat, climbed aboard and began throwing our precious supplies overboard in order to save the boat and the motors from sinking to the ocean floor. Once sufficient weight had been jettisoned, we chose the absolute necessities for building and everything else was unloaded and left behind. Now, with the boat much lighter and safer, we were able to continue our journey to Lili with greatly improved chances of arriving there alive. Fortunately, with Don and Heather's arrival came the introduction of much stricter guidelines that would prevent a recurrence of incidents like these. Don was also skilled in mechanical repair work and very capably maintained our two 25 horsepower outboard motors.

With Don's boat expertise we were all set. But the McCalls, like the rest of us, would take eleven months after every four years to

FIRE ON OUR BOAT

return home for what is now called 'home assignment'. That meant that during those times our 'boat captain' would not be there to pilot us on that perilous sea journey. Just before Don left for Australia, it was decided that I should take over the captaincy of our newest boat, a marine ply catamaran. Fortunately, as a result of frequently travelling with Don, I had picked up a few clues on how to run our boat but I don't think I had ever consciously considered that one day it would become my entire responsibility. Had I realised that, I'm certain I would have paid a lot more attention but in my optimism, I was convinced that we would soon have a mission plane, making boat travel a thing of the past. Obviously I was far too optimistic.

A month or so before the McCalls departed for home, Don suggested that I take the boat out on the 260km return journey to Tobelo without him. I dubbed it my 'trial by fire', not realising at the time just how accurately that phrase would describe what was to transpire just a few kilometres shy of our Lili home. Our Indonesian co-workers, Chris and his very pregnant wife Otari, accompanied me with Chris' younger brother Sammy on what was a very uneventful trip out to town. Even getting through the coral reefs went well, a leg of the trip that could be hazardous at low tide. However, the return trip was to cause me enough trauma for a lifetime.

In order to save money on fuel, Don had modified our petrol outboard motors to run on the less combustible but significantly cheaper kerosene. We would get them started on petrol and then, once running and warmed up, switch them over to kerosene. The problem was that if the motor stalled while running on kerosene, it was then necessary to empty it all from the carburettor before trying to restart the motor on petrol. Failure to do this would leave you pulling on the starter cord for hours to no avail. Refilling fuel tanks and cleaning out the carburettor was always fun in rough seas.

To complicate matters, the constant removal and re-installation of a small fuel hose to empty out any remaining kerosene in the carburettor bowl had caused a crack to develop in the hose. That slit was about to get much worse. On this, my maiden voyage as Captain, the split hose began to spray petrol all over the very hot motor. What made matters so much worse was that we had a three quarters full plastic jerry-can of petrol securely tied down right beside that motor. For some time, we remained blissfully unaware that beneath the motor cover, petrol was being sprayed all over the motor. To compound the danger, occasional sparks were tracking down the side of a salt-encrusted spark plug. Now, although he's not Don McCall, even Captain Sharpe should have known that this was a recipe for a disaster. Sure enough, that spark eventually ignited the petrol and suddenly the secret goings on under the motor cover led to a full-blown crisis. In no time the motor was engulfed in flames. The fire also engulfed the plastic jerry-can which still contained about fifteen litres of highly flammable petrol.

This explosive situation created panic, and predictably, all kinds of dramatic thoughts ran through my mind. I immediately yelled to a very pregnant Otari to get to the bow as far away as possible from the burning motor and told her to get ready to dive into the water. Next, I told Sammy to get the fire extinguisher. But, as if in a bad comedy movie, a spray bottle containing a mixture of oil and kerosene that we used to spray down the motors in preparation for storage was accidentally confused for the extinguisher. This only added more fuel to the fire! Grabbing hold of the jerry-can handle I frantically began trying to pull it away from contact with the flames, absolutely certain that an explosion was imminent that would result in terrible burns or worse.

Here now was another occasion where I desperately cried out to God for His protection. Eventually, after frantically pulling to loosen the ropes that tethered the jerry-can in its place, I was able to wrestle it beyond the reach of the flames. Chris then unclipped the outboard motor cover and filled it with sea water, dousing the motor and finally extinguishing the fire. With the fire now out, we all just sat in stunned silence, physically and emotionally exhausted. We were unable to move, such was the trauma we had all just experienced. Eventually, with our hearts back in our chests, we started up one of the two inboard motors and slowly limped on home. What a start to my job as our boat captain! I did not relish the thought that, for the next year, this would be one of my team roles.

On another occasion, when Don was thankfully in charge, we encountered a storm that whipped up huge waves. They crashed over the boat, absolutely drenching us all. The combination of massive waves and a small boat isn't a good one, and to make matters worse, our small children were also on board. We often worried what impact these trips might have on them but on one occasion, as the waves poured over us, our little Anita, totally unaware of the danger we were in, said to Anita Miles, 'Aunty Anita, aren't we having such fun?'

During my year as boat captain, I would make a number of trips out to Tobelo and back, some of which were reasonably enjoyable experiences but others were in very rough conditions that could have easily resulted in terrible consequences. Thank God the latter never eventuated.

THE TUGUTIL

Construction of a marine ply catamaran that replaced the single hull boat which sank during our landing on the shore at Lili

Our family, Chris and his brother Sammy travelling on a beautiful calm sea

- 11 -
FREDI'S STORY

> But Jesus said, 'Let the little children come to me and do not hinder them, for to such belongs the kingdom of Heaven.'
>
> MATTHEW 19:14

Our first contact with Fredi was when we saw a pitiful looking little boy standing on the beach in Lili, hair all matted from pus that leaked from his terribly infected ears. Diving deep in the river to hunt fish with his little spear gun was one way that Fredi could get food to satisfy his hunger. It was most likely that this activity had caused his eardrums to burst, resulting in the painful ear infections he had somehow learned to live with. The resulting stench from his ears caused people living nearby to avoid coming too close to Fredi which only reinforced his feelings of rejection.

Fredi's mother had run off with a man from a village many kilometres south of Lili. Fredi couldn't believe that she would desert him, his brothers and their father and so each day waited expectantly for her to return. Sadly that day never eventuated and so his father Minggusu toiled to care for himself and his three young boys in an attempt to keep their little family together. But Fredi constantly lived with the sadness of rejection, convinced that he was a worthless piece of rubbish.

After our initial arrival in Lili, the medical needs of the people quickly became obvious and Fredi was one of those cases. The people in Lili had no access to any kind of medical assistance and so would call on their witch doctors in the hope that they could appease or manipulate the evil spirits that they believed caused their sicknesses. Keith administered a child's course of antibiotics and some nice smelling shampoo and that was all it took to make a world of difference to this forlorn little character. Having someone actually take an interest in him and display a measure of care for him significantly impacted his little life. Years later, God would dramatically take hold of Fredi's life and use him as a wonderfully gifted church planter and Bible co-translator. He would one day work with Keith Miles to see God's Word translated into the heart language of his people.

But Fredi wasn't the only one feeling worthless. Many of the Tugutil were aware that there were people living in the surrounding villages who considered them to be half-human and half-animal. In research we had carried out prior to entering the tribe, we had heard stories about the Tugutil killing animals with their bare hands and then tearing the flesh apart to eat the meat raw. Along with these stories came claims that they were dangerous killers and people who certainly should be feared. Many people told us that we were crazy to think we could live among them and not end up dead. But suspecting that many of the tales we had heard must have been gross exaggerations, we hoped that the reported dangers involved in living among them had also been overdone. It would be many years later that the true extent of the actual danger we were in would be revealed to us.

- 12 -
'HAPPY THE WAY THEY ARE'

There is no fear in love, but perfect love casts out fear. For fear has to do with punishment, and whoever fears has not been perfected in love.

1 JOHN 4:18

There is no doubt that in the early days of living among the people there were aspects of their lifestyle that did seem on the surface rather idyllic. But the longer we lived among them, the more we came to understand the fear that controlled much of their thinking. Their supply of food from the jungle included deer and pig meat, sago, sweet potatoes and another root vegetable, corn, fish, a couple of varieties of nuts, a limited supply of fruit and sugarcane. Actually all of these foods were in fairly limited supply. As well as this food scarcity, many also had to contend with food taboos that further restricted their already limited diet. There were times we heard of people living on nothing but sugarcane for days on end. Without any way to clean their teeth, the sugarcane had disastrous effects. Many people's teeth were in the process of decaying or had already completely rotted away. Several years later, we would convince a dentist from Ambon to accompany us into Lili during which time she and her assistant pulled hundreds of the people's half rotten teeth.

THE TUGUTIL

But occasional hunger wasn't the only source of pain, hardship and suffering for the tribal people. Malaria and tuberculosis (TB) were rife. The Tugutil believed that a fever was the result of an evil spirit cooking the sick person's intestines in preparation for eating them. This explained why people ran high temperatures and then sometimes died. The spirits or 'tokatas' were at work and unless the witchdoctors could appease that particular spirit, the person would soon die.

Childbirth also held many fears for the women and justifiably so. Many had witnessed women die in childbirth and we heard stories of young girls being in labour for days unable to deliver their baby and dying terrible deaths. If a mother did die and the living baby was still connected by the umbilical cord, then both would be buried together, despite the baby being alive.

The Tugutil believed that multiple births were due to an evil spirit impregnating the mother. They believed that a man could only father one child and so the other baby must therefore be the offspring of an interfering evil spirit. If allowed to live, the unwanted twin would eventually grow up into a grotesque person who would turn on the people, killing them. Therefore it would be necessary to identify which baby was the evil one and that baby would then be left out to die of exposure and starvation. In the event that it was not clear which child should die, then both should be left to die. This practice was considered essential for the wellbeing of the tribe.

Anita Miles spoke to one mother who described the heartache she experienced as she listened to the ever weakening cries of her starving child. Unable to bear them any longer, she ran to feed the child only to be reprimanded by the older women and forced to again leave the baby to die. Seeing our twins and the obvious fact that both were beautiful, loving little girls, caused them to question this aspect of their world view and, as a result, the next set of twins girls born up to our north were both permitted to live.

So high was the infant mortality rate that parents would delay naming their children until they were around five years of age. By then they figured that they stood a fairly good chance of remaining alive despite all the difficulties and sickness that their harsh lifestyle would throw at them.

On one occasion, a young girl's mother-in-law reasoned that her daughter-in-law's family must be the cause of her son's terminal sickness. She proceeded to send the girl back to her parents but insisted on keeping her young baby. With the baby now separated from her mother's milk supply, the grandmother walked to the village and purchased a can of sweetened condensed milk. She then added water until the condensed milk looked similar in appearance to mother's milk and tried to feed this to the baby. When we became aware of the situation, we immediately ordered cans of baby formula but unfortunately they wouldn't arrive for weeks. Knowing this, we tried to organise some of the breast feeding mums in our area to feed the baby but according to their beliefs, a mother of a baby of one sex must not feed a baby of the opposite sex. They believed that doing this would certainly send the wet nurses' milk sour, resulting in the starvation of their own babies. All the mothers we pleaded with had boy babies and so refused to provide milk and in no time, this gorgeous little girl starved to death.

These stories present a serious challenge to those people who believe that tribal people should not be introduced to ideas and practices that are culturally alien to them. This is faulty thinking. It assumes that tribal people must have their notions of truth validated at all costs, even if their lives would significantly improve as a result of receiving new knowledge. This age-old problem comes back to having no trustworthy standard of truth. If there is no absolute truth against which to assess a particular practice, then whatever notion a person or a group decides is held to be true, whether it is right or not. The result is fear, ignorance, pain and death. People who wish to do away with a perfect standard of absolute truth – God's standard - really need to think that proposition through to its logical consequence. Applying that philosophy to the situation of that starving infant would totally legitimise needless suffering and fear, and a painful and pointless death. Those people should ask that young mum - who is now a Christian - what she thinks of the tribal people's version of 'truth' that resulted in the senseless loss of her beautiful little daughter.

The setting of pig traps was one common means of hunting, but the Tugutils' worldview dictated that the spirits would be angry if they checked their traps more often than every third day. Therefore, should a trap spear a pig or deer the night after it was set, then the animal would not be retrieved for another two days. Three days in the tropical heat would send the meat bad, resulting in food poisoning for those who would consume it… but rotten or not, the spirits would also be angry if all the meat wasn't consumed. These were just some of beliefs that constantly weighed on the minds of the Tugutil people, trapping them in burdensome practices that led to conflict, misery, suffering and death. The more we understood this, the more we saw that they were certainly not happy the way they were! It also highlighted the fact that we could do all the socio-economic development work under the sun, but if there wasn't a fundamental change in their belief system or worldview, then not a whole lot would ever change for them.

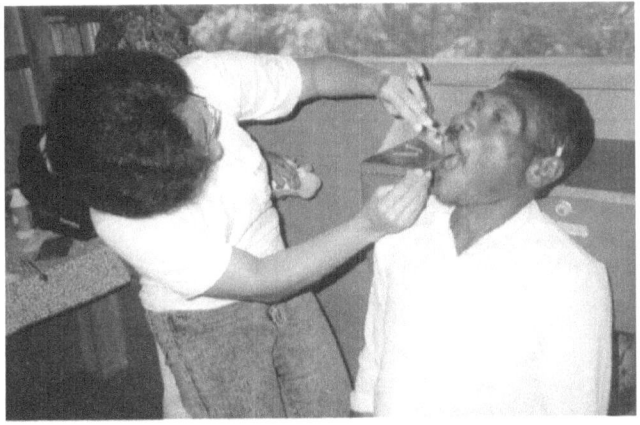

We flew in a dentist and her assistant from
Ambon who pulled around 200 teeth

- 13 -
THE 'TOKATAS'

Come to me, all who labour and are heavy laden, and I will give you rest.

MATTHEW 11:28

As the years in Lili passed by, our insights into the people's worldview progressively grew. This was particularly true of the role that the 'tokatas' (evil spirits) played in their lives. Animistic people believe that ancestral spirits inhabit inanimate objects such as trees, large rocks and fields along with certain birds and animals. Consequently, they spend their lives in fear, attempting to manipulate and appease these spirits in order to avoid the calamities that they believe will certainly befall them should they neglect to do so. The Tugutil believed that tokatas could possess people. Operating from their dwelling place within a possessed individual, the spirits could eat the intestines of anyone who ventured too near. We discovered that this view was not limited to the tribal people but was also widely held in many of the villages dotted along the coastline. Most of these villages had churches, but sadly the professing 'Christians' continued to hold onto much of their old animistic world view. They attempted to mingle their animistic beliefs with aspects of Christian teaching. This resulted in a superstitious mish-mash and a misunderstanding of the liberating power of the Gospel.

Early in 1987, our co-workers Keith and Anita Miles were visited by an older couple who came asking for help. They had fled from one of these coastal villages. Their village had branded the woman as possessed by a tokata and were now convinced that she had eaten several people in the village, resulting in their deaths. Now the villagers lived in fear of the woman and the only solution in their eyes was to have her killed. The couple knew that it was only a matter of time until she would be poisoned or disposed of by some other means and so they had come to our co-workers pleading for help. But the news of their coming had preceded them and the Tugutil living in our area were also convinced that the woman was dangerous and was to be avoided at all costs.

It is interesting to note how the accusation arises that a certain person has become a tokata. Someone – and the initiator's identity is usually vague at best – reportedly sees the suspect in the process of eating a victim's intestines. This story begins to circulate and is heard by the children who then run and scream when the 'tokata' approaches. Then, as soon as there is a death, the people are convinced that it is the work of the suspect, whose life has been made a complete misery. Being shunned and continually slandered, they have no alternative but to separate themselves from the community and live a life of isolation. To remain living as part of the community is to choose death.

Sadly, this label wasn't only applied to adults. Three young sisters who regularly visited us had been ostracised because their grandmother lived with the stigma of being considered a tokata, and so along with her husband, she had been forced to live on a deserted part of the coastline. One day, the girls told us that they were no longer able to visit us. A young, newly married girl whose house they passed by when coming to see us had begun calling them tokatas. We knew these sweet girls well and were disgusted by the accusation. But our attempts to dispel and change these deeply ingrained beliefs with logic were doomed to certain failure. And so their grandmother's tragic life of loneliness, fear and absolute misery could now so easily became theirs. Such life situations among animistic people simply continue on until the grave. What a contrast this sad existence is in comparison to the new birth, new life and renewed mind offered by Jesus Christ. Encountering their living, personal Saviour and being indwelt by the glorious Comforter, the Holy Spirit, was clearly the only hope for change among the Tugutil people. Exactly one year later we would commence teaching the incredible message that God was to use to bring about that liberating and life-giving change.

- 14 -
WILL WE EVER GET THIS LANGUAGE?

> Come, let us go down and there confuse their language, so that they may not understand one another's speech.
>
> GENESIS 11:7

Reports that the Indonesian language was a comparatively easy one to learn was a major factor in our choice of Indonesia as our preferred field of service. Betty showed good aptitude in language school; my language school report however said I would need to work exceptionally hard but that I should succeed due to my high level of motivation. We were also told that the tribal languages were of the same Austronesian language family as the Indonesian national language so, once somewhat proficient in Indonesian, you would then have a good start on the tribal languages – or so they said.

We had no idea that over in the eastern province of Maluku there was an incredibly difficult tongue from the Papuan family of languages waiting to exasperate the daylights out of us. To master it would greatly challenge even our very gifted language learner and team linguist, Keith Miles. After about three years of struggling with language learning, we began to wonder what on earth we had struck. Keith then produced the following sample text that demonstrates the incredible complexity of 'bahasa', Tobelo's system of affixation – or adding prefixes and suffixes to base words. His chart took the verb 'to do' = 'diai' and progressively added affixes. Look at how it impacts meaning:

diai (verb stem) = to do / to make
i**diai** = it is made
na**diai** = you make it
no**tiai** = you make it level
nohi**tiai** = you make it right
nohi**diai**o = you are making another one
noma**diai** = you make for yourself
nomahi**diai** = you get ready to leave
nomihido**diai** = you nurse her back to health
nomimakete**diai** = you (the witchdoctor) are spitting medicine (betel nut juice) on the sick lady
konomido**diai**ua = you do not care about her
konomahido**diai**ua = you are being reckless (not careful)
konomahido**diai**okaua = you don't know how to be careful anymore
konomahido**diai**ikakauali = you probably fell down there again (because you are not careful)
konomahido**diai**ikakauahie = you have not learnt to protect yourself yet in that situation, have you?
Kohomahiketehido**diai**ikauali = we will never help one another out in this situation ever again

As someone who didn't even find learning Indonesian particularly easy, I fully grasped the massive effort that would be required if we were to learn this language. On occasions I felt like throwing in the towel and once even asked our field leaders if they would

WILL WE EVER GET THIS LANGUAGE?

Keith Miles, our team linguist working on
language lessons with Habiana

simply allow us to teach in Indonesian and have Chris translate the teaching into the people's language. Chris had grown up in a village where a dialect of the language had been spoken by some of the residents, and so he had quickly reached fluency in the language. Being monolingual speakers, none of the Tugutil understood any Indonesian. Wisely, our leadership refused our request, knowing how problematic working through a translator can be. And how do you then disciple people and establish a church through a translator? With their culture expressing itself through their heart language and the two being so deeply interwoven, how would we ever truly understand their worldview without learning their language?

So, discouraged, but still very determined that the Tugutil would be given the opportunity to hear God's story, we prayed that God would give us the strength and persistence to keep pressing on. God's answer was simply for us to be faithful one day at a time and by His grace, just keep pressing on. Every so often, one of the people would comment that we were doing so much better at speaking their language and these times were a huge encouragement.

But then someone would say, 'Even my little children already know this language!'

At times like that I felt like replying, 'Well, why can't you speak English yet? Even my little girls already can!', but I resisted the urge.

One of the most important attributes of a good language learner is the ability to laugh along with others when they are cracking up over your blunders in the language. We were certainly providing the best entertainment they had ever had and especially on those occasions when we slaughtered their language. But today, we are ever so thankful that we persisted, unaware that it would still be more than two years before, instead of them always being our teachers, we could finally share something of incredible importance with them.

Practising language with our visitors

- 15 -
BUILDING THE AIRSTRIP

> As for you, always be sober minded, endure suffering, do the work of an evangelist, fulfil your ministry.
>
> 2 TIMOTHY 4:5

After experiencing a number of horrific boat trips in and out of Lili, including one sinking and other occasions when we were forced to pull in and camp overnight on the beach, we had decided that we would only send Naomi and Anita to school once we had a functioning airstrip. But establishing an airstrip would be much easier said than done. It first involved gaining government approval, which our wonderful Indonesian office team were able to secure. Our virgin jungle backyard was home to some of the biggest trees we had ever seen. Clearing those trees to build an airstrip wouldn't just be a matter of chain sawing them down. It would necessitate extracting the root system of each tree as well. Failure to do this would result in the airstrip sinking in places where the roots gradually rotted underground. A plane's wheels hitting one of those soft spots could have fatal consequences. The task would be an impossible one without machinery and so we prayed to God - yet again - to intervene.

One morning, the answer to this dilemma appeared on the

Miles' front doorstep. A lumber company, who had previously been reluctant to enter the area due to their fear of the tribal people, were aware that we had moved in and were actually surviving the experience. They therefore decided that it was safe for them to enter the area and avail themselves of the huge trees just waiting to be harvested and sent off to plywood mills in Japan, an incredibly profitable venture. After meeting with the lumber company officials, we were able to negotiate certain conditions to protect the tribal people's nut trees, a variety normally taken for timber. We received some assurance that alcohol would not be distributed to these people who had not been previously exposed to it. We also gave a strong warning about the deadly consequences of touching their women and warned them not to fell trees on the graves of their ancestors. But gaining their assistance to build the airstrip was a long and arduous task due to the easy access they had to the huge trees growing in abundance along the coastline. The profitability of their exercise would always take priority over giving assistance to us. But every so often there would be a positive response to my pleas for help and a very old D7 Caterpillar bulldozer would turn up on-site. Daily for six months we worked away, gradually seeing more and more of our 700 metre long runway taking shape.

Building the airstrip. Just look at the root system of this monster tree that was pushed over by the bulldozer

BUILDING THE AIRSTRIP

Eventually, our pilot came in by boat and gave the nod of approval to our jungle airstrip. Now we could send our girls to school without exposing them to the dangers of travelling by sea... or so we thought. In anticipation of the strip being completed, we decided to go ahead and enrol our eight- year-old daughters for the upcoming school year. Kevin Miles had told them many exciting stories about school life and what a wonderful adventure it would be.

Despite the airstrip not yet being completed, we decided that we should take a trip to Palu in Central Sulawesi to introduce Naomi and Anita to the mission's elementary school, dorm parents and teachers. Getting there would involve a combination of one, or possibly two boat trips and two, possibly three plane flights. The lumber company informed us that their much larger boat would be going out to town and we were welcome to accompany them for the first leg of the journey. But their boat ended up being delayed by three days due to wild seas. Eventually arriving in town, we discovered that there was a series of special government meetings taking place and that all planes had been commandeered for this event, resulting in another three days stranded in Tobelo.

After boarding another boat and travelling overnight to Ternate, we found that the same meetings had caused a huge passenger backlog there. We eventually arrived at the school in Palu eleven days later. Having a mission plane would have cut the travel time down to one or two days. Well the day did come when we felt that we could make plans to bring the plane in and this happened to be perfectly timed for our taking the girls to begin their time at school. But the airstrip, still devoid of grass, was only usable after several hot, dry days had hardened the surface. As the day approached for the initial landing, spasmodic showers came through the area and we grew increasingly nervous about the possibility of heavy rain rendering the airstrip unusable.

The decision was made to do the 130km boat trip out to town rather than risk being delayed for the start of school because of being forced to cancel the plane due to heavy rain. A couple of hours' bus ride north of Tobelo was the small town of Galela and its old coral based Japanese World War Two airstrip that was used by a government-owned airline's nineteen-seater plane. It was decided that our pilot would meet us there for the five hour flight to the school. We arrived in Tobelo two days prior but on the day we were to be picked up from Galela, our airstrip ended up being hard enough for a plane to land in our absence. We actually could have flown out of Lili after all, saving us the boat trip and several extra days of travel. I do wish I could've been there to witness that long-anticipated first landing of a plane on the airstrip we had worked so hard to build.

- 16 -
THE HARDEST THING

And he said to all, 'If anyone would come after me, let him deny himself and take up his cross daily and follow me...'

LUKE 9:23

Our daughters, Naomi and Anita, had often sat in awe as Kevin Miles related stories from his days at our mission school in Palu, Central Sulawesi. Kevin, an outstanding, captivating and extremely funny storyteller, made school seem so wonderful that the girls just couldn't wait to experience this fascinating place and meet the people for themselves. Our visit to check the school out went really well so we went ahead and enrolled Naomi and Anita to commence third grade in line with the American schooling system. Years later when she was in high school, Anita would write the following essay, which she submitted as an assignment for grading. Shortly after handing it in to be marked, she saw her English teacher reading it - in tears. Anita's essay is reproduced below, unedited.

I was almost eight years old when my parents decided to send us to Palu, a little city in Central Sulawesi. Our mission school there was called Wera Falls Academy. This decision was met with both excitement and great anticipation by my sister and I.

Being our first time, Mum and Dad travelled with us to school to help get us settled in. It was a four hour flight (when we could fly in our mission plane) to get from our tribal location to the town about an hour's drive from the school. I knew that the pain Mum felt about us leaving was indescribable. Weeks before we were due to leave, I would hear her anguished sobs. Dad's low, loving voice, in the room across from my sister's and mine, would comfort her with a prayer: 'Lord, we commit our two, precious little girls into your hands. We know that you love them even more than we do. Teach them that You are always there even though we aren't.'

Little did I know how these simple prayers my parents prayed would become an ever-present comfort to them and a protective shield around both my sister and I. Little did we all know the positive effect that this decision would have on both our lives.

The day before we were due to move into the dorm, the idea of school became not so exotic as the reality sank in that we would not be seeing Mum and Dad for months at a time. I can remember saying 'good bye' to my mother at the guest house as she fought to be brave in front of us. No longer was I the excited little girl I had been a few days ago. I clung desperately to my Mum, not wanting the last few minutes of time to elapse without her knowing how much I loved her. Tears streamed down my tiny face as I begged her to buy me an air plane ticket to return home with them. I promised profusely to be good forever ... if they would just never leave me.

Dad picked up my sobbing form; my arms still outstretched towards my Mum, and carried me to the car. I remember seeing Mum dash from the room, all composure shattered, her body racked with deep, heartbroken sobs. The whole way, my sister and I sat quietly in the warm comfort of our dear Daddy's arms, enjoying his voice as he told us about all the fun we were going to have. Mostly, however, we relished in the nearness of him. His presence was so dear to us at that moment.

The trip was all too quick and before I knew it, we had arrived at the school. I overheard Dad murmur quietly to the taxi driver, telling him to wait and that he wouldn't be long. My little heart started to pound. I had to do something to make him forget that he had to go back. 'I'll be really good. Yes, that will work.' I reasoned to myself, 'If Daddy forgets to go then he will miss the plane and have to stay with us.'

Dad basically had to do all the unpacking for me. I was too busy telling him what fun 'we' were going to have here. Little did Dad know that he was included in my plans. By the end of unpacking, we had both brightened considerably, me, because I was sure that my plans for detaining the man of my life were working, and Dad, because he was encouraged by my renewed enthusiasm.

I remember as if it were yesterday, how my sister and I had sat, one on each knee and listened to his soft, low voice that we loved and knew so well. He read us the story of the little boy with five loaves and two fishes. Somehow, in my mind, I knew without a doubt, that this would be the last time in a long while that we would sit like this together, plan or no plan.

As if reading my mind, I felt myself being gently pushed off his lap. Tears came unbidden to my eyes, streaming down my face. Our little hands clutched tightly to each of his legs. I looked up into the face of my dear father. No longer was there the controlled look of calm about him, but his face was shrouded in pain and heart ache. I could see the doubt slamming into him from all sides, 'How can I leave my two little girls here. They don't know anyone. They have never been away from us for longer than a night. Lord, what am I doing?' No longer was my Dad the comforter, but rather the expression on his face was a scream for reassurance that he was doing the right thing.

Hysterics set in as Dad's leaving became reality. He bent down and pulled me close, just holding me there as my little body shook with sobs. He didn't say a word. My pleas became choked as I struggled for relief from the pain crying brought to my throat, and stomach, but it was the ache inside my heart that was the most unbearable.

My father, as if using the last ounce of his strength, desperately tore our clinging hands away. He stumbled blindly to the awaiting taxi. He never looked back. He never said good-bye. Yet I never questioned his love. For the first and last time in my life, I saw the tears running down my father's face. I saw his body heave with his suppressed grief. I saw his tear streaked face peering out the window, his lips moving in a silent prayer for strength and courage. I knew he was and would be praying daily for his two little girls far away across the sea.

Naomi and Anita's dorm parents, Don and Charlene Alderman, were the most caring, wonderful couple. They knew exactly what to do in that situation in order to make the girls feel so very loved and secure. This was true of each of the couples who had charge of our precious daughters during their time away at our mission's primary and secondary school, something for which we are so incredibly thankful. Our girls look back on their entire mission school experience with such wonderfully positive memories. Sadly though, their positive experience has not been the case for all missionary kids who have spent time at mission and secular boarding schools around the world.

- 17 -
OUR UNDEPENDABLE AIRSTRIP

> Blessed be the God and Father of our Lord Jesus Christ, the Father of mercies and God of all comfort, who comforts us in all our affliction, so that we may be able to comfort those who are in any affliction, with the comfort with which we ourselves are comforted by God.
>
> 2 CORINTHIANS 1:3-4

I can't begin to describe the excitement we felt on each occasion as we anticipated the girls' coming home for their school breaks. It was on their return from their second semester of school that, as their arrival day approached, we began looking at the sky and praying that the weather would be fine for the plane's arrival. For the week prior to their scheduled landing, we would wake and immediately look out to find the sky clear and blue. With the airstrip still not covered by grass and with no way to pack the soil down sufficiently hard, the strip remained a strictly dry weather strip. I remember being down at the river the afternoon before they were to leave for home and expressing my fear that rain was coming as the clouds began to build up and grow increasingly dark. The next day, the plane departed with our girls and two other children from another island. They were to be dropped off first and the plane would stay overnight there and then do the one hour forty-five minute flight into Lili the following morning.

Despite the cloud build up, no rain fell and that night we

looked out unable to see a single star in the sky. Things did not look good but we wanted to trust God for a fine morning. That night, at about 10 pm we heard the first drops of rain on our iron roof. It wasn't long before that sound soon became a thundering noise as the skies opened up. Soon we were in the middle of a massive tropical downpour that was to go on throughout the night and into the next morning when the girls were due to arrive. Around 8 am, Don McCall and I walked down to the strip and immediately saw that there was no way a plane could ever land on what now look like a sticky, muddy mess. Words can't begin to describe how gutted and totally discouraged I felt. *Why had God allowed it to remain fine right up until the night before their planned arrival?* If it had rained before they left the school, we could have made other arrangements but now the girls were half way home and stranded. To be honest I felt like God had pulled off a huge double cross, some kind of rotten trick. Wasn't life difficult enough without this kind of thing happening? I thought, *you can do this to me, but not to our girls.*

Returning to the house I passed on the devastating news about the airstrip to Betty. *How would we now get our girls home?* Our boat was out of action so I couldn't get out to town to go and get them. The situation was one where all the control had been taken completely out of our hands. As we sat in our house about as discouraged as it is possible to be, Betty took the girls' little Casio keyboard and began to pick out the notes for the hymn *Great is Thy Faithfulness*. It was then that God spoke so clearly to me, just as He had already been reassuring Betty.

'Who loves those girls so much more than you do? Who is the One ultimately in control here? Why don't you give them to me, the One who knows what is best for them rather than trying to control it all yourself?'

'Okay God', I finally agreed. 'Yes, You do know what's best for them and we do know that we can trust You to love and protect them far, far better than we ever can.'

After my crying out to God, it was back to the SSB radio where our pilot, still on the island of Taliabu, was connecting with a couple who were Bible translation consultants. They were planning to come in and do a check on the translation work that had been completed to that stage. After some frantic rearranging of their schedule, a plan was hatched that would have them fly to Galela and meet up with our pilot and the girls. Larry, Jill and our girls would then travel to Tobelo and from there, come together by charted boat into our location. We prayed for good seas and within a couple of days we welcomed them all safely into Lili. The girls were quick to report that they had had a fantastic and fun filled trip and even got to see their boat run into a pylon in the harbour as they were leaving Tobelo. Betty and I could have coped just fine without hearing that part of the story. Yet again, in the midst of all our fears and turmoil, we saw the goodness and faithfulness of God displayed in bringing our precious girls safely home to us.

- 18 -
CHALLENGES AND DISCOURAGEMENT

> Give justice to the weak and the fatherless; maintain the
> right of the afflicted and the destitute.
>
> PSALM 82:3

Prior to our arrival, the fearsome reputation of the Tugutil had discouraged others from moving into the area for the purpose of clearing land to plant coconut trees. As mentioned, many thought we were absolutely crazy for moving in to live among them but once it was apparent that we had not only survived but appeared to have been well accepted, some then felt it would be good for them to also move on in and get a share of the fertile land around the Lili River. Realising the disservice we may have done the people in inadvertently opening up the area to these outsiders, we immediately travelled to Buli to see the 'Camat' (local government head man) and requested a letter restricting the farming of the Lili valley exclusively to the Tugutil people.

The Camat, a Roman Catholic, was very understanding of the situation and immediately issued the requested letter. Now it would be our job to confront any outsiders and turn them away so that this prime land would remain available only to the tribal people. This certainly didn't make us popular with those living in coastal villages nearby who were being refused permission to farm in Lili. It wasn't long before stories began to circulate about us in the hope that we would be removed from the area. These attacks on our characters included attempts to discredit us with the tribal people. One story had us living in Lili because Australia, New Zealand (Don's home) and America were now so full of people, that we had come to take their land in Lili. Another claimed we were going to steal their children and whisk them off as slaves to sell overseas. Another weird story claimed that we were there to open a shoe factory. There were probably many other stories that thankfully, we didn't get to hear.

The most serious accusation levelled against us claimed that we were inciting the tribal people to go and kill the headman of the village to our north, and this one eventually reached the authorities. This earned us a visit from the Indonesian security service. After an exhaustive investigation, they discovered that the reverse was in fact true. We had actually been responsible for preventing violent acts against outsiders when the tribal people had been provoked and had wanted to take matters into their own hands. Those who had levelled the false claims against us were the ones who eventually ended up in big trouble with the Indonesian authorities and we were permitted to continue on with their blessing. After that, the stories promptly ceased. It would be some years before another situation would mend the bad feeling some people had towards us for our role in preventing their exploitation of Lili's land and resources.

- 19 -
THE DEADLY MEASLES EPIDEMIC

> And we know that for those who love God all things work together for good, for those who are called according to his purpose.
>
> ROMANS 8:28

It was January 3, 1988, and we were now only three months away from finally beginning to teach the Tugutil through the main stories of the Bible. For a number of weeks we'd been hearing reports of a deadly measles epidemic getting progressively closer to Lili. This prompted us to encourage the tribal people to avoid going near the coastal villages where we expected the next outbreaks of the highly contagious disease soon to occur. However, when it did arrive, the folk from those villages came to us for medical help. One man, who had lost his daughter the day before, decided that this time he would bypass the village shaman and bring his very sick son directly to us. Tragically, his nine year old boy died in his arms just as he was lifting him out of the boat they'd arrived in. The next day saw an influx of panicked village people bringing their children to us accompanied by adults stricken with the highly contagious virus. Many had also visited the local shaman only to see further deterioration in their condition and so now they viewed us as their very last hope.

It soon became obvious that most of those who had contracted measles were developing complications, usually pneumonia. This weakened their resistance to malaria which was rampant at the time and the combination of all three was deadly. In discussing this tragic situation, we decided the best course of action was for us to pack up the boat with medical supplies and go up to the village which was now being severely impacted. This would remove the need for those who were terribly sick to have to make the long trip down to us and also allow the Tugutil to remain somewhat isolated from the epidemic.

Early the next morning we loaded up the boat and Don, Chris, Betty and I set off on the 30 minute ride to the village of Dorosago. Upon our arrival, we were met by the village headman who ushered us into his house and there we were given the use of two rooms. It soon became obvious that the line of sick people stretched out of sight and by the end of that day over 400 people would have passed through the door desperately seeking our help.

With the crowd ever growing, we quickly realised that we would need to develop a system that reduced Betty's work load to the areas that most required her nursing expertise. So in order to cope with the vast numbers, Don, Chris and I did whatever we could to help expedite the process while Betty listened to their lungs for pneumonia and determined exactly what medication should be given. Most required antibiotics and medication for the malaria that was rampant at the time. At the end of the day, we all returned home totally exhausted but very satisfied that we had undoubtedly saved numerous lives that day.

Almost a month later, we were again visited by another village headman, this time from the somewhat smaller village to our south. He arrived requesting that we come and do exactly what we had previously done in Dorosago. He told us of three deaths that had just occurred and of the fear that now gripped the village as more and more contracted the virus. And so, once again, we repeated what we had previously done, only this time with fewer people. Later on, we would be thrilled with reports from both villages that not one of the hundreds we had treated had died as a result of the epidemic. Our intervention went a long way toward re-establishing good relationships with some of the village people who had formerly resented our presence after we had lobbied the government to restrict the fertile Lili valley for farming exclusively by the Tugutil. Once again, God was able to bring something good out of this tragic circumstance.

- 20 -
OUR MEDICAL PROGRAM DILEMMA

> Let every person be subject to the governing authorities. For there is no authority except from God, and those that exist have been instituted by God.
>
> ROMANS 13:1

It was a lazy Sunday afternoon when our little CB radio suddenly blurted out the very familiar words,

'Are you by, John or Betty … are you by?' Reaching for the radio, I replied,

'Yes, go ahead Keith'. In a tone that conveyed the seriousness of the situation, Keith proceeded to explain that a government delegation had arrived at his house accusing us of running an unauthorised medical program that must be immediately shut down. The group comprised a doctor who was the director of the regional health department and several government-employed rural health workers. Any thoughts of having a relaxing Sunday afternoon now totally gone, we quickly scrambled to tidy ourselves up into a state befitting meeting government officials and scurried down the trail to Keith and Anita's house, about a fifteen minute walk away. As Betty operated our team's medical program, she would certainly be the one to whom most of their questions and accusations would be directed.

THE TUGUTIL

Arriving at the house, we were greeted by the sight of a number of men sipping hot sweet tea and eating biscuits that Anita Miles had prepared. Receiving delegations, often very high ranking officials from Jakarta, was not uncommon but we usually had prior warning and hence the opportunity to prepare for their coming. Not so this time. The expression on Keith's face as he introduced our guests relayed to us the concern he was feeling and that this could have dire ramifications for our work in Lili. Betty and I wondered what else they had communicated with him that we were unaware of, and later Keith would describe the hostile manner in which their complaints and accusations were conveyed.

Introductions completed and tea cups almost empty, except for the culturally obligatory amount left in the cup indicating that they had had sufficient to drink, the questioning began. It didn't take long to work out that this visit had arisen from complaints by the rural medical workers. People in the area were coming to us from further and further away rather than utilising their services. Unfortunately back in those days, these medical workers were only given limited training and were not well resourced, so many people they treated simply didn't get better. On the other hand, almost all the people Betty treated went on to recover. In fact, apart from the deaths of several newborns; we didn't have a death for about the first four years of our time in Lili. We would discover how this fact may well have saved our lives in those early years, in light of one strongly held belief of the people.

As word of people's successful recoveries spread, so more and more people wanted to bypass the health workers and instead come to the Lili 'hospital' and see the Australian 'doctor' lady. The delegation saw this as a serious problem but actually so did we. Betty could only be stretched so far in meeting the medical needs

OUR MEDICAL PROGRAM DILEMMA

of people from miles around and was already burning out treating our local tribal people and the Muslim village an hour's walk south, whilst coping with everything else she had on her plate.

The first question from the health department's doctor was to establish if any of us were indeed qualified to run a program of this nature. Betty's qualifications as a trained registered nurse appeared to totally satisfy that requirement and the questioning then moved to the medical complaints Betty was treating and how she was going about doing that. Fortunately, Betty had kept meticulous records for every patient including their complaint, treatment, prescribed medication and dates of visits, cost of medication and any other relevant information. A thorough inspection of these records resulted in a total change of attitude on the part of the doctor.

No longer was there any hostility or opposition to what Betty was doing. After inspecting the medical house built for us with funds from World Vision, the doctor, obviously greatly impressed by what he was seeing, actually invited Betty to visit him at his hospital. He then made an offer of medical equipment so that she could further expand the scope of our medical program. He had come with the intention of closing us down and now was keen to not only see the program continued, but also expanded. I'm sure this total change of attitude on the doctor's part did not impress the health workers, who were probably thinking that they had shot themselves in the foot by even raising the issue.

But any expansion of the program was the last thing we wanted. Previously, a couple of us had entertained the idea of assisting the lumber company with medical care as a way of possibly reaching them, totally oblivious to the impact that would have on Betty. 'Yes, let's totally burn her out, only in half the time!'

Eventually the suggestion was made from our side that in order to protect the health workers' livelihoods, we get a letter from the health department restricting those who could use our medical house to only those who lived within a certain radius of Lili. This then got the health workers back on side and restricted the scope of the program to a more manageable size. That way we all got what we wanted ... except maybe for the doctor who left desiring to see the program he had come to terminate further expanded.

No doubt, God greatly used Betty and her medical work in Lili to show His love for the Tugutil and the many others who were recipients of her dedicated and loving care. After our departure from the tribe to take up a leadership position in Ambon, Heather McCall would take on that responsibility. Possibly Heather's greatest medical challenge came when she was called upon to successfully nurse a young man through tetanus and back to full health.

Betty treating a young man who had been shot in the back with an arrow

- 21 -
CHURCH - THE STRONGEST TABOO

> They exchanged the truth about God for a lie and
> worshipped and served the creature rather than the Creator,
> who is blessed forever! Amen.
>
> ROMANS 1:25

The Tugutil were a people who had been deceived by the prince of this world - Satan - and their worldview was distorted by many of his destructive lies and deceptions. One of those lies was the belief that if they ever entered a church or had any contact with it, a member of the offending party's family would die. This belief had kept the Tugutil isolated from the church group that had congregations in many coastal villages north and south of the Lili River where the Tugutil lived their semi-nomadic lifestyle. In some ways this actually worked out to be a good thing as the churches in the area were plagued by syncretism or the mixing of animism with aspects of Christianity. We had heard stories that years before we arrived, a couple from that church had moved into the area and ordered the people to assist them in building a church they were to attend every Sunday. The people reasoned that to do this would eventually see the whole tribe wiped out and so it would be far better to permanently remove the couple, which had promptly happened.

After more than five years of studying the language and culture of the people, we would finally be ready to teach God's Word but, prior to that, we were aware of their taboo against the church. In 1986, our nearest neighbour, Ula, had gone hunting alone and failed to return home. His body was later discovered in the jungle. Apparently a few months prior to his death, Ula's youngest brother and his eldest son had gone on a hunting trip and had called in at a lumber company camp. There they were invited to join a birthday celebration which, unbeknownst to them would also involve a short church service as the family was 'Christian'. Inadvertently they had now attended a church service, something they must never do according to the taboo. Ula's death would be directly attributed to the breaking of this taboo. After all those years of coming to grips with their complex language, would this reinforcement of their taboo make them unwilling to ever listen to God's Word? We had to face the fact that they may never choose to listen to the message we were working so hard to be able to deliver.

As the time to teach the tribe drew near, we began to talk to the people about this wonderful message that we desperately wanted to share with them. We explained that, although it was good that we could help them in practical ways, and especially with the medical program, we had actually come for a far more important reason. The message we had come to share was such an important story that we had left our dearly loved families and friends back home in order to bring the message to them. We had willingly suffered sicknesses like malaria, dengue fever, black water fever, tropical ulcers and other illnesses as well as undergoing dangerous boat trips and separation from our children while they were away at school. But we did these things because the God who made

CHURCH - THE STRONGEST TABOO

all that they saw around them was a communicator who wanted them to hear His wonderful story.

One day, a young man named Ausu asked me if this would be 'church', as they had a taboo against church and therefore wouldn't be able to attend. I thought about it for a moment and then asked him to tell me their understanding of this 'church' that they couldn't attend. He replied that they have 'church' in the villages along the coast on Sundays so I replied,

'We'll tell the story on Monday, Wednesday and Friday mornings'. He also said they needed to get all dressed up to go to church in good clothes to which I replied,

'No need to get dressed up. Just come as you are, even if it's straight from working in your garden. You can hear this story dressed in dirty clothes or dressed in a loin cloth if you like'. He then said they needed to pay money, which I imagined was referring to the church offering. I replied,

'You won't pay anything for this'. Next came the comment that you could not smoke or chew and spit betel nut in church. I reassured him that whatever they did when they listened to their own stories being told, they should feel perfectly free to do when they listened to God's story. He said they sing and talk to God. I told him that there would be no singing or praying, only the telling of God's story. Finally he told how they would get upset in the church if the babies urinated on the floor through the sarongs that cradled their little naked bodies. Again, I assured him that it would be absolutely no problem if they did that when we told this story. After all, the place where we were hoping to use just had a dirt floor.

I did emphasise that we would be using the book that they used in the Indonesian church called the 'Alkitab' (Bible) as that

THE TUGUTIL

was the source of the story. I also made sure that they understood that regardless of whether they believed the story was true or not, nothing would stop them from being our dear friends. Ausu then made my day by replying that he thought it would be fine for them to attend the story if it was presented like that. To our amazement, about 250 other tribe members turned up for the first day of teaching.

- 22 -
CAN THEY HEAR US?

And a voice came out of the cloud, saying, 'This is my Son, my Chosen One; listen to him!

LUKE 9:35

A swell of excitement had begun to grow among the Tugutil people as we had been preparing to begin the teaching of God's story. Our field consultants required that we first prepare one third of our lessons or stories before commencing delivery of this wonderful narrative. Being ahead in our planning would ensure a buffer in the event of unforeseen interruptions with lesson preparation and Scripture translation that might disrupt the continuity of the story. With the exception of one brief break for a translation check, we would keep teaching three mornings every week until the final story of Christ's ascension to Heaven in the book of Acts.

We had arranged for the construction of a large corrugated iron-roofed structure, hoping that the people would choose it as the logical location for the telling of God's story. We expressed our willingness to tell the story out in the open under the boiling hot sun if that's what they preferred, but they all wholeheartedly agreed that a shelter would be ideal. We had thought that the structure would easily accommodate everyone who might attend, but in fact we had to extend the roof on both sides to get everyone under cover from the scorching sun and tropical downpours. Of the approximately 250 people who gathered on the first day, most would continue attending until the story's completion six months later.

Modelling the teaching house after their own houses meant that there were no walls. This allowed entry to dogs, chickens and noisy roosters and one day, a snake. Of course, most of the women came with their babies and small children, none of whom had previously ever attended any gathering anything like this before. After our first day of yelling our lungs out in order to be heard over the dog fights, roosters crowing, kids screaming and women chatting, we decided to purchase a 12-volt amplification system. This made a huge difference although we still had the dogs and chickens to contend with.

One morning we had a rooster chasing a hen that was desperately looking for a spot to lay its egg. The poor bird flew up into the roof rafters of what we now called 'the teaching house' and promptly dropped its egg. Fortunately, at that very moment, the man sitting directly below looked up, cupped his hands and caught the egg, to the great amusement of the gathering. We joked that he got a double blessing that morning - the story and lunch!

Not long into the teaching, some of the ladies began complaining that they were having difficulty following the story, since one of the extremely extroverted, gregarious ladies frequently insisted on talking as the story was being told. So Betty approached the woman and asked why she wasn't interested in hearing God's story.

'No' came the reply, 'I am listening to the story. I can answer most of the questions you ask us after each part of the story'. This woman obviously had the ability to somehow follow the gist of the story while simultaneously chatting away but, the other ladies, like most of us, could only listen to one thing at a time. Betty, who had formed a close friendship with this woman, gently helped her understand that although she was getting the message, her talking was distracting others from hearing God's amazing story. Throughout the entire presentation of the story, we made sure we asked questions after every session to ensure that what the people were hearing was in fact an accurate representation of the story we were intending to pass on to them. Checking their comprehension certainly helped us to expose any parts of the story that lacked clarity. The talkative woman, on her own initiative, chose to be one of the last to arrive so that she could position herself away from those to whom she couldn't help but talk. She continued to quietly listen and was one of the first to fully comprehend the wonderful saving work that Jesus did on her behalf.

- 23 -
THE TRANSFORMATION BEGINS

> Come now, let us reason together, says the Lord: though
> your sins are like scarlet, they shall be as white as snow;
> though they are like crimson, they shall become like wool.
>
> ISAIAH 1:18

The evangelising of the Tugutil people of Lili was a long process. It first involved teaching key Old Testament stories before telling the story of the life and saving work of Jesus. We first taught the creation of the angels, Lucifer's rebellion and subsequent fall. We taught how a third of the angels followed Satan in his rebellion against his Maker and that these fallen angels were the demons or tokatas that played such a big role in the Tugutil's lives.

This set the scene for the temptation of Eve in the garden. After picturing the wonder of a perfectly created world and then the creation of Adam and Eve, the people were guided to an understanding of the temptation and fall of man, as the first man and woman on Earth chose to believe Satan's lies rather than the truth revealed by their Creator God. Suddenly, things became very different because of the decision Adam and Eve made - causing devastating consequences for them, their descendants and all of Creation. Now they understood the origins of death and why life is such a constant struggle for survival. But this all powerful

God was also a gracious God and immediately promised to send a Redeemer from 'the offspring of the woman' to redeem fallen Creation from this terrible mess we were all now in. The people listened intently as we told them how this 'offspring' would destroy Satan, who from the time of the first sin in the Garden onwards, ruled the world. Genesis 3:15 was the verse we shared - the first of many promises that the Tugutil would begin to cling to, of a coming Redeemer for the world and for the Tugutil. Thus we helped the people begin their quest to discover whether or not this Redeemer had come. If He had come, who was He? Where was He? When did He come? Where is He today? And how do we come to know Him?

The completion of the teaching of Genesis 3 happened to coincide with the time of the year when the Tugutil would leave the village in order to make rice offerings to the spirits to ensure a good harvest. Actually, the people ate very little rice in comparison to most Indonesians, but of the little they did grow, the first fruits would need to be offered to the spirits. This spirit festival continued on for several days and nights and involved the pounding of drums and dancing to summon the spirits. This war dance, called the 'cakalele' involved the men stomping and twirling with a machete in one hand and a shield in the other. As part of gaining an understanding of how they viewed life, we had attended one of these festivals as observers. Thus we knew that their attendance would mean

The 'cakalele' war dance

THE TRANSFORMATION BEGINS

them being absent for several important parts of God's story. We therefore decided to stop telling the story until all those involved had returned home. This way they would not miss any of the unfolding narrative. Not once did we ever try to discourage them from leaving to attend their festivals or condemn any part of their belief system. So, when we relayed this to them, we were in no way prepared for their amazing response.

One of the key men, Taunu, began by saying that they were not going to have their festival this year. In fact they were probably never going to have it again. He went on to tell us how they had crushed up the spirit rocks used to protect them when they travelled, and had thrown them away. Along with other fetish objects relating to the spirits, they were thrown into the river where they could never be retrieved. In many different tribes, using this same approach to evangelism, the disposal of these kinds of objects related to spirit worship often happens after the completion of the story. But we had never heard of this happening so early on in the story telling process. As a team we had purposefully never condemned nor condoned the way they lived as it was directly related to their spirit world.

Our thinking was that, if any permanent change was to come about in their lives, it would have to be a work of God's Spirit and not simply out of conformity to what we saw as acceptable belief and behaviour. With that in mind, we were also careful to avoid condemning any of their beliefs or actions we found objectionable. God's story alone and the work of His Spirit would have to be the catalyst for change and that change must come from within them. Our job would be to teach God's Word and the Holy Spirit's job would be to use the truths found in God's word to help them decide what needed to be changed in their belief systems and practices and what needed to be retained and possibly even strengthened.

Imagine our surprise when Taunu totally amazed us again. Upon hearing the story of Satan's deception of Eve, he had realised that they too had been deceived into following Satan and his demons. But now we had come to tell them about the one true God. They had talked and decided that they no longer wanted anything to do with Satan but instead wanted to follow the one true God who they were now hearing about for the very first time in their very own language. This happened after teaching just the first three chapters of the Bible! Thus began a journey that would eventually lead them to discover Jesus Christ - God's ultimate answer to mankind's devastating dilemma.

- 24 -
NOT ACADEMY AWARD CALIBRE, BUT THEY GOT THE POINT

> Abraham ... took the ram and sacrificed it as a burnt offering in place of his son.
>
> GENESIS 22:13B (NIV)

As the Tugutil people would discover, the Old Testament provides a wonderful foundation for foreshadowing what is fully revealed later in the New Testament, that is, how God puts mankind right with Himself through the death, burial and resurrection of Jesus. One key illustration is the sacrificial system God instituted among the Israelites. The Tugutil would eventually see that the sacrificial lamb is a key component of the Gospel. Just as the sacrificed animal's blood was shed and then the body burned, so too the person offering the sacrifice deserved exactly the same death. The people saw that it was God who dictated the way mankind must approach Him if they were to avoid that same certain fate. They saw that simply trying to come to Him the way *we* think is best, no matter how sincerely, just doesn't cut it with God.

The story of Cain and Abel reinforced the concept of a substitute. An innocent animal would die in the place of guilty, sinful man. For, as the Bible says, 'The person who sins will die' and 'all have sinned and fall short of the glory of God.' Both Cain and Abel brought sacrifices but God accepted Abel's offering and rejected Cain's. One brother came on God's terms and the other came according to his own reasoning. Abel came believing God in faith and Cain came without faith and without an acceptable sacrifice. If we are to be accepted by God we simply have to come to Him, His way! And that's exactly the message that the story we were telling them conveyed. God's story would progressively follow this concept of animal sacrifice but they would also discover that animal sacrifice could only cover sin for a single time – it was a temporary covering, only a shadow of the One who God promised would come as a 'once and for all' payment for sin that provided never-ending forgiveness.

In time, the people saw Abraham introduced into the story and God testing him by telling Him to sacrifice his son, Isaac. We acted this out for them and they were absolutely glued to each moment of the drama. Later one of the men would testify that, because of the taboo, he was almost too terrified to attend the story. But once he saw the first dramatisation of a particular incident, he simply couldn't bear the thought of missing any future performances. On occasions such as this where the dramas included some scary, violent moments, the children didn't recognise that we were acting and actually feared that someone was in fact about to be killed. We had to clarify that no one would be harmed in any of the dramatisations we would do.

As the actor playing Abraham stood there leaning over Isaac with the knife, the Tugutil wondered what Abraham would do. We told the story of how He obeyed God and was prepared to plunge the knife into his much loved son, believing that, should he kill Isaac, God would restore his life. This would be necessary if

Abraham was to have descendants that were eventually to become the great nation promised by God. But now the question in the minds of the people was would Abraham really believe God's promise to the extent that he would actually kill his son? Yes, that's what he set about doing and so Abraham willingly prepared an altar and placed Isaac, upon it, ready to slay him. We emphasised the fact that Abraham's solid belief in God's promise made him righteous in God's sight. Just as the knife was about to be plunged into Isaac, the people saw God intervening and preventing Abraham from killing his son. God then provided a ram caught by its horns in nearby bushes and it was sacrificed in Isaac's place. The people could see that this was a substitutionary sacrifice - a perfect picture of what they would later see Jesus do for them.

Another drama we performed that registered a massive reaction from the people was the treatment of Jesus at the hands of the Roman soldiers after His arrest. Don had made up a crown of huge, razor sharp thorns and we came up with a whip in order to demonstrate the shocking ordeal Jesus underwent. One of the tribal guys played Jesus and Chris took the role of the Roman soldier, mocking and spitting on Jesus and then flogging him with the whip. As soon as the teaching session was over, a delegation of men fronted up at Chris and Otari's house demanding to see Chris. They then asked him how he could possibly do those terrible things to Jesus when Jesus had not done one single thing wrong in His entire life. How could anyone possibly treat Jesus like that? He was the wonderful, perfect, spotless Son of God who was full of grace and truth. Chris assured them that he was only acting out the part so that they could better appreciate exactly what Jesus went through for all of us.

'Okay' they replied. 'But just don't ever do that again!'

The hunger of the people to hear more of the story was brought home to us one morning after the river height had risen to a level far too dangerous for even adult men to attempt a crossing. As a good number of the men, women and children coming to hear the story had to cross the river in order to attend, we talked among ourselves on our radios and decided that we should cancel the teaching that day. We felt sure that all those from across the river would also decide that the river crossing was far too dangerous and simply return home. However, it wasn't all that long until the radio burst into life.

It was Chris informing us that all the folk from across the river had arrived, all sopping wet and wondering where we were. After hurrying down to the teaching house, we had a quick meeting and decided to inform them that if the river ever reached anywhere near that level again, the teaching would be postponed.

'After all,' I said to them, 'how tragic it would be if someone lost their life attempting to get across the flooded river. How terrible we would feel knowing that such a thing had happened because they were coming to hear us tell them the story.' Amazingly, that statement elicited quite a response and brought one of the older women to her feet. Ongo Polulu proceeded to inform us that they had not had God's story available to them for such a long, long time and now that they finally had the opportunity to hear it in their very own language, they didn't want to miss a thing. We were instructed not to worry about them getting across the flooded river. Our only concern was to make certain that we turned up each teaching day so that they could continue to hear the remainder of God's story. They would make sure that they were present and so should we!

- 25 -
O TORO'S DEATH

'O death, where is your victory? O death, where is your sting?'

1 CORINTHIANS 15:55

We continued telling all the main Old Testament stories so that the people would see the story as one cohesive, unfolding narrative passed on from God to them. Besides simply telling the story, we also pointed out the truths that God was teaching us through those stories, their purpose and meaning in the bigger picture of Scripture and the redemption plan. This captivated their attention. They loved the dramas we performed and the pictures we showed to accompany each story. These teaching aids helped to ensure that we conveyed an accurate understanding of the message that God wanted all of them to understand.

Immediately after completing the story about Jacob's dream of a ladder between Heaven and Earth, a picture of God making a way for mankind to come back to Himself, we noticed the absence of one of our keenest listeners. It would be the last story that a man by the name of O Toro was ever able to attend. Prior to our starting the teaching, O Toro had purposely avoided having much contact with us and seemed fairly suspicious of us. At times we would hear about his children being sick and encourage him to come for medicine but that rarely happened. However, when he himself was sick he came to us, hopeful that our medicine along with the efforts of his witchdoctor brother, Puhuhu, would bring about a speedy cure. He was not a person that we would have expected to come and hear the story we so desperately wanted them all to hear.

About the time we were due to begin teaching, one of O Toro's very small children died and he and his family came out to Lili for the burial. There he noticed a large group of people gathering at the teaching house and that made him curious as to what was going on. Of course they were gathering together to hear the very first instalment of God's story. O Toro decided to attend too, mainly to see what all the fuss was about. From that day on he consistently attended and sat right up front with his wife and children, glued to the message that he was hearing for the very first time. Most nights he would come to one of our houses where he could sit and listen to recordings of the stories we were telling them each Monday, Wednesday and Friday mornings in their own heart language.

One day, O Toro's absence was noted and we were informed by his wife that he was indeed very sick. Betty and I called in on our way home from our time with the people and it was obvious that he had malaria and possibly something else besides. Treatment was immediately begun but O Toro didn't improve at all and, in fact, his condition seemed to be deteriorating. With no improvement, we arranged to have him moved to a house much closer to ours in order to check on him more regularly. Soon he was unable to keep down the oral medication Betty was giving him. One day he did manage to keep some medicine down but it was only moments later that his witchdoctor brother arrived with a concoction that he insisted O Toro drink. Betty's friend, Edenge, ran to our house informing us that the mixture would certainly make him vomit up the medication he had just taken – medicine he desperately needed to absorb. I immediately raced across to them and pleaded that Puhuhu, the witchdoctor, at least delay giving his concoction to O Toro until our medicine had some opportunity to get into his system. Then, if he still so desired, he could have him drink the 'medicine' he had prepared. But ignoring my pleas, Puhuhu immediately insisted that O Toro drink the concoction. O Toro complied with his brother's request, and immediately threw up the tablets that hadn't yet had time to dissolve in his stomach. My frustration was obvious to Puhuhu and all those looking on. This embarrassed his brother, resulting in a 'loss of face'. He immediately departed the scene.

We prayed for God to once more do His miraculous healing work as we had seen Him do to save the lives of two other critically ill people before. One of them was a lady, Ongo Hubu, who gave birth to a beautiful little girl we named 'Ajaibi' or 'miracle'. The mother's placenta did not deliver for five days after the birth of the little girl and all the people who had witnessed other similar cases were sure she would die. But Hubu didn't even run a fever and eventually the placenta did deliver without incident. The other instance was a young man, Ngodoro, who was shot in the back with an arrow. The arrow passed right through his body, protruding out just a couple of inches above his navel. Ngodoro certainly would have died without miraculous intervention. But in both of these cases we pleaded with God for healing and He graciously answered our prayers, demonstrating to the people His great power, compassion and love.

But in O Toro's case, it soon became apparent that he was not improving and that death was quickly approaching. We quickly decided that I should jump ahead to the fulfilment of the last story he had heard taught. I reminded him of what he had learnt about God and sin and how we were all separated from our Maker because of it. I went on to explain that the One promised in the book of Genesis who would become that ladder back to God for us, had in fact already come a long, long time ago. His name was Jesus (O Yesusu) and I then proceeded to explain the wonderful Gospel story. Being way ahead in lesson preparation was so helpful as it gave me key terms in the language for the biblical words I would need to use in my explanation to this dying man.

O Toro saw that God, who because of His justice must judge sinful man, had already poured that judgement out on His own Son on the cross and then raised Him from the dead. If O Toro truly believed that, his debt to God for sin was now paid in full by Jesus. O Toro's face, which had only reflected the excruciating pain he was experiencing, began to beam with delight. We could see that now he was a child of God with absolutely nothing to fear from death. O Toro summoned his family and instructed them not to do what every other Tugutil family had done after the death of an adult - destroy the deceased's house. The Tugutil believed that if the house was demolished, the person's evil spirit wouldn't be able to return and locate their spouse in order to take them to be with the departed loved one. We ourselves had previously been encouraged to flee our home when our closest neighbour died. But instead, we told the people that we were not afraid and would just stay put. Betty explained,

'Once we can speak your language really well, we will tell you why.' Her friend responded by saying that she hoped that time wasn't far away.

Don and I stayed with O Toro and his family until the early hours of the morning when he finally fell unconscious. Earlier that night, O Toro was asking his son-in-law, O Life (pronounced 'Lee Fay') if 'they' had come. I had assumed he was speaking of his brothers, but O Life explained that he was referring to the three angels that he believed were coming to get him and in the morning take him to be with Jesus. O Toro passed away around 7 am the next morning.

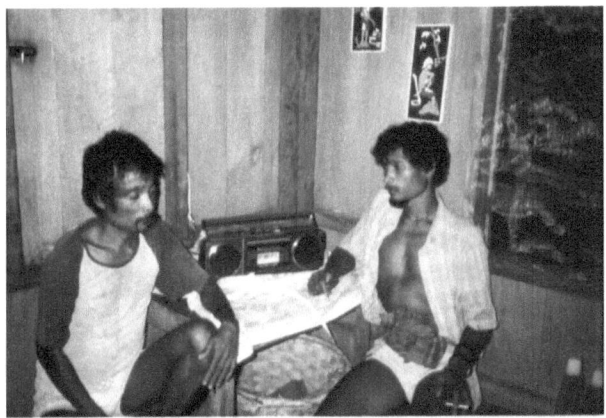

O Toro (left) and Muru sitting in our house listening to recordings of the portions of the story

- 26 -
IN THE MIDDLE OF A SPIRITUAL BATTLE

> For we do not wrestle against flesh and blood, but against
> the rulers, against the authorities, against the cosmic powers
> over this present darkness, against the spiritual forces of evil
> in the Heavenly places.
>
> EPHESIANS 6:12

Upon hearing of O Toro's death, his witchdoctor brother seized upon the opportunity to link O Toro's death to the breaking of Tugutil taboo against Christianity. He clearly needed to vent his intense anger and grief over the loss of his brother, so he channelled all his emotion and energy into hatred toward us, me in particular. My last contact with him up until this point had been the time that he had lost face over the medicine incident. Chris, who was living nearer the coast, warned me on the radio that he could hear Puhuhu coming through the jungle, screaming threats. Soon afterwards we heard the same threats and then saw him emerge from the bushes, along with his teenage son and son-in-law, all three fully armed and heading towards our house.

We quickly sent the girls over to Don and Heather's just before the trio stalked into our house, still brandishing their weapons. This was the very first occasion that anyone had ever done this. Until now, they had always left their weapons up against a tree in our front yard to indicate their peaceful intent. Betty, thinking of the countless hours I had spent with Puhuhu and all that we both had done to assist him and his family, was now fed up with all his carry on. She marched out to meet them. Convinced that I may well be in a life-threatening predicament, I felt like heading in the opposite direction but I somehow worked up the courage, especially with Betty already out there, to confront my very angry friend. Don then appeared on the scene and we were able to explain how heartbroken and saddened we were at his dear brother's death. Eventually things calmed down after Betty got them a cup of sweet tea and something to eat and then, as quickly as they appeared, they were gone. We were left in little doubt that this was yet another miraculous intervention by God.

Initially, Puhuhu had been very supportive of us telling God's story but the further into it that we progressed, the more he could see his power and control over the people as a shaman being gradually eroded. The very next day, as Don continued teaching the story, Puhuhu arrived on the scene and positioned himself directly in front of Don - totally taking over the proceedings. He began by telling everyone that one person had now died because of the broken taboo and that he would start committing revenge killings if anyone else should die. Therefore, he insisted that everyone must immediately cease listening and follow him. He intended to take them to the beach where they would build shelters and he would teach them the ways of their ancestors every Monday, Wednesday and Friday morning.

We estimated that about forty adults and children left with him that morning and the remainder of us sat there rather shell-shocked. Then some of the remaining people approached us saying that some of Puhuhu's relatives who had not accompanied him might place the rest of us in danger should they become sick and die. They advised that, for the safety of all concerned including ourselves, we should encourage these people to stop coming to our sessions. Our response to this was to clarify that we would not restrict anyone from hearing the story and that if the attendance of Puhuhu's relatives made them fearful, then maybe they themselves might have to consider not coming. But not one of those who remained allowed their fear to stop them coming and it was only a week before one young couple, O Je and his wife, told Puhuhu that they would be returning to hear more of God's story. Puhuhu told them that, should they do so, they would both be dead within a week. Calmly, O Je replied,

'We would rather be dead and know the true God than be alive and bound up by all these lies from our ancestors!' O Je and his wife were the first of a large procession of people who returned to hear the completion of God's wonderfully liberating story.

- 27 -
GIVING OF THE LAW

> So then the law was our guardian until Christ came, in order that we might be justified by faith.
>
> GALATIANS 3:24

One of the most incredible moments we experienced as we shared the Bible story chronologically occurred during the lesson on the giving of the Ten Commandments in Exodus 20. The Tugutil were a fairly self-righteous people who tended to blame outsiders for all the troubles in their world, rather than accepting any personal responsibility. I remember asking one man if the people ever did anything wrong. He replied,

'No, but those people in the villages north and south of us sure do.' We often wondered how they would react to receiving the gospel, realising that they would first have to acknowledge the bad news about themselves before being able to accept the good news of what Christ had done for them. The time eventually came when we began the lesson on the giving of the Ten Commandments at Mount Sinai. We carefully taught each of the Commandments, one by one. As we did so, we explained what each law actually entailed for the Israelites and how, in giving the law, God was revealing His holiness and perfect character. We explained that mankind had a

THE TUGUTIL

huge problem. A perfect God could only live with perfect people and this law was going to show us all just how terribly imperfect we all are. We also talked about our own personal failure to perfectly keep these laws, and how our imperfection would become even more apparent later in the story. This of course was referring to the teaching Jesus would give, clarifying that even the thought of breaking the commandments was just as bad as the act in God's sight.

In order to visually demonstrate this lesson, I took a brand new, white, spotless t-shirt, still in its plastic cover - a rarity in the high humidity and often muddy conditions in Lili. I held up the t-shirt, telling the people that this represented the holiness of God, who is absolutely perfect and without sin. I then lifted up an old, white rag that I had made extra dirty, and used it to represent mankind, all of whom had broken God's perfect law. To my surprise, one of the men, Perus, suddenly rose to his feet and told me that the dirty rag didn't represent him. My initial response was to think that I had grossly offended him and would soon incur his anger for my offensive statement about his condition before God. But it was actually the opposite reaction that he was about to convey. Perus announced loudly,

'If that dirty rag is supposed to represent me, then you need to make it really, really dirty!' So I proceeded to dunk the rag in a muddy puddle beside the teaching house. I then noticed a pile of cow manure. The Tugutil people hate cow excrement and give it a very wide berth when passing by any on the jungle trails. Knowing this, I dabbed the rag in the manure and again held it up. Perus then made an incredible statement that I will never forget.

'Now that rag looks like me' he said. 'When I compare myself to what I now know God is like, I'm just like that very filthy rag!' Others in the crowd nodded in agreement, also acknowledging that they were desperately needy sinners whose goodness fell incredibly short of the standard of perfection that God required in order for man to gain His acceptance. God's Spirit was applying His law to prepare their hearts for the good news of a Saviour who had died for them so that they could freely receive His gift of perfect righteousness as their very own.

Chris beginning to tell the story that would continue for six months. Don (right) unfolding more of the story

- 28 -
FUN MOMENTS DURING THE TEACHING

> For everything there is a season, and a time for every matter under Heaven ... a time to weep, and a time to laugh; a time to mourn, and a time to dance.
>
> ECCLESIASTES 3:1; 3:4

As Don, Chris and I taught the Tugutil people the stories of the Old Testament, we certainly saw some humorous responses coming from the people. One couple in particular come to mind. The story in question was about the children of Israel complaining as they wandered in the wilderness for forty years. We looked at the story of the serpents in the desert biting and killing the people (Numbers 21: 4-8). God told Moses to make a bronze serpent and raise it up on a pole. Those who had been bitten were to look to the serpent on the pole and their lives would be saved. In teaching the life of Christ they would discover that this was a picture of Jesus taking our sin upon Himself and being lifted up nailed to a cross. All who looked to Him in faith would be saved. Well, the Tugutil already knew by now that God was long-suffering, but through this story they also got the message that God would only tolerate a sinful, complaining spirit for so long and this certainly had an impact on them.

Living along the coast in the tropics, the temperature often sat at around 33 degrees Celsius and the humidity was often around 80–90%. Any real physical exertion at all resulted in us quickly being drenched in perspiration. It was on one such day that a group of people arrived at our house and, after giving the usual greeting, I said something to the effect that it was stinking hot today. One of the men responded,

'Yes, it is hot but if God wants it to be hot then I'm fine with it being hot. I'm not complaining. You can complain if you want to, but I'm not.' He wasn't going to be like those complaining children of Israel and the inference was that I should think twice about my complaining attitude as well!

Another humorous reaction came with the teaching of the story of Pharaoh's response to Moses' request that the children of Israel be released out of their slavery in Egypt where they had been for the past 400 years. The Tugutil understood Pharaoh's reluctance to lose his free labour force, but they expected that once the plagues commenced, he would quickly relent and set them free. But plague after plague passed and Pharaoh's heart just grew harder and harder. We explained that Pharaoh himself initially hardened his own heart and then God further hardened his heart in order to more clearly reveal His power and glory as He brought the people out of their bondage in Egypt. Well, despite God's involvement in hardening Pharaoh's heart, Pharaoh was given the name 'Rock Head' by the people. From that time on, everyone who displayed any arrogance or stubbornness was given the title 'Pharaoh the Rock Head'. They just couldn't believe that anyone would be so stupid to resist God. This guy had to be an absolute idiot to ignore and challenge the Almighty God! One man - a real larrikin - even adopted the name for himself and many willingly used his new name when talking about him or even directly to him. His wife loved it and thought it most appropriate.

- 29 -
THE STORY DRAWS TO A CLOSE

> And there is salvation in no one else, for there is no other name under Heaven given among men by which we must be saved.
>
> ACTS 4:12

After four months of stories from the Old Testament we finally reached the story of the One to whom the entire Old Testament pointed – the Lord, Jesus Christ. We told the people of his birth in Bethlehem, just one of the many fulfilled prophecies they had heard from the Old Testament. Regarding these prophecies, we had displayed a list of the things that would have to happen in the life of the promised Messiah. Then, as we told the story of his life from the Gospels, they saw each one progressively fulfilled. Yes indeed, Jesus was the One God promised He would send to deliver us from the terrible mess we were in.

The Tugutil saw that Jesus lived a life that demonstrated His power and authority over sickness, death, demons and nature. He had the authority to call people to follow Him. They saw His spotless, perfect character. Although human, Jesus was the perfect, sinless Son of God. Just as in the Old Testament a perfect lamb without defect was sacrificed in place of sinners, Jesus qualified as the only One who could stand in our place. His sinlessness meant that He alone was qualified to rescue us.

We told the people the story about Jesus sleeping in the boat during the violent storm on the Sea of Galilee. We explained that the disciples were absolutely beside themselves with fear that their boat would sink in the storm, and I asked the people a question.

'What do you think Jesus will do?' One man stood up and said, without hesitation,

'I think He'll just tell the wind and the waves to stop and they will have to do what He says.' 'Why do you say that?' I asked, amazed at his perceptiveness.

'Because remember when you told us about God creating the world? You told us that God the Father, the Son and the Holy Spirit were present at Creation. Well, we now know that Jesus is God the Son and God simply spoke the world into existence. Therefore, Jesus will simply have to speak to the wind and the waves and they will have to obey Him.' And of course that's exactly what happened.

We continued through the New Testament, telling the people how Jesus challenged and upset the religious establishment and how, after three years of ministry, his followers saw the perfect Lamb of God, whom they had come to love, arrested and taken before Pilate, the Roman governor. We unfolded the events leading up to Jesus' death carefully, telling the people that Pilate attempted to convince the crowd that Jesus didn't deserve death but the people, fired up by the religious leaders, demanded his crucifixion. The Jewish religious leaders had decided that He must be condemned in order that they might be free of his influence. After all, He was claiming to be God and in claiming to be able to forgive sin, He was a blasphemer. This only added to the fury of the Jewish religious leaders whom Jesus had exposed as hypocrites, snakes and blind guides.

The Tugutil received detailed teaching about the crucifixion – we acted out the scenes in which Jesus was taken away, enduring a horrific beating at the hands of the Roman soldiers and was then led away to be crucified. We dramatised these aspects of the story so that the people had some idea of the terrible ordeal Jesus underwent as the sacrificial Lamb of God who took upon Himself the sin of the world. They vividly saw the truth – that He stood in their place and received the full anger of God for their sins and ours - past, present and future. Now, we explained, all who trusted Him would never, ever have to face God's anger and condemnation themselves. This was wonderful news to the Tugutil. There were people in the gathering whose faces simply shone for days with the wonder of knowing that God loved them unconditionally and could accept them as His sons and daughters because of what Christ has done.

I reminded the people of the dirty rag that I'd used as a symbol of mankind's sin and the spotlessly clean T-shirt that represented Jesus' holiness and purity. I told them how God had looked upon their sin and, because justice is part of His nature and character, had no choice but to judge and condemn them. But then taking the dirty rag, I wrapped it up in the spotlessly clean cloth that represented Christ. In this way, I demonstrated how a holy God could accept them, even in their present sinful condition. They saw how God covers each and every person who places their trust in Him with Christ's perfect righteousness, and that God views such believers as being as righteous as His own Son. God now saw them holy and righteous 'in Christ'.

Many of the Tugutil grasped the wonderful truth that they too could enjoy a relationship with God because Jesus' righteousness was imputed to all who trusted in Him and His finished saving work. They realised with joy that salvation has absolutely nothing to do with them becoming good enough for God. Trying to find acceptance through their good works would be an impossible task as God's pass mark was no less than absolute perfection. The majority of the Tugutil now knew that Christ was God's one and only way and those dear people clung on tightly to that wonderful truth.

- 30 -
MORE FUN WITH OUR TUGUTIL FRIENDS

> And I am sure of this, that he who began a good work in
> you will bring it to completion at the day of Jesus Christ.
>
> PHILIPPIANS 1:6

In the years following the coming of the gospel, each Christmas we would do the Christmas story and have the people act it out as a drama. When we asked about the possibility of having one of the numerous babies in the area play the baby Jesus, the response came back as an emphatic 'NO!' None of their children could ever be anywhere near good enough to play the part of the baby Jesus. He was perfect and they knew that their babies were certainly not! They insisted that a doll belonging to Rebecca or Esther McCall or our Naomi or Anita would need to take that part!

The play, which attracted many outsiders, went off really well and the initial group of actors then became the consulting experts and directors for the new actors in subsequent Christmas plays. And of course, each time it had to be done *exactly* as they had performed it on that first occasion - or else.

Another humorous incident occurred after some of the new believers had been spreading unsubstantiated stories about certain people they knew. I thought it was a good opportunity to address the issue of gossip at church. After sharing a few relevant Bible verses, I told a story about someone who had picked a few coconuts from his garden and on the way home had decided to take a short cut through another man's garden. As he exited the garden, someone noticed him with his bunch of coconuts and immediately assumed that he had taken them from that garden. He told someone else who then passed on an exaggerated version of the story to others. Within no time at all, the poor man who'd simply taken a shortcut home was being accused of stealing a wagon full of coconuts when in fact, he hadn't taken a single one. The people saw the obvious injustice in the story. Later that day, I saw one of the main culprits who had fuelled the gossiping problem and asked him what he thought of the morning's message.

'I'm so glad you told that story,' he responded.

'So did the story impact your thinking at all,' I asked?

'Oh it sure did! Now when I need coconuts, I'm going to get mine at night so that no one will start spreading false stories about me,' he asserted. It goes without saying that a little more clarification of the salient point of my illustration was immediately forthcoming.

After we completed telling the Gospel story, almost all of those who attended testified that they had now put their faith in Jesus Christ. It was a natural transition to begin meeting on Sunday mornings and we would once again repeat the entire narrative to bring further clarity to any who still lacked a clear understanding. Now all who believed were a part of this brand new church and they loved meeting together. There is no doubt that God did amazing things to confirm to the Tugutil people that He was real and that He was looking after them. We encouraged them to share their news about these happenings during a testimony time to finish off the church service. I remember a mother testifying that she was prompted to pick up her very small child and move her just before a huge tree fell on the very spot at which the child had been sitting. Another testimony was shared about two young boys who were out fishing in a small canoe when a shark came up out of the water. It attacked one of the boys, its teeth narrowly missing his body and clamping instead onto his well-worn shorts, ripping them completely off him. Both boys were able to paddle safely back to the shore unharmed, despite the one with no pants being very embarrassed!

We had to smile when the testimony time became an opportunity for some women to embarrass their husbands for failing to step up to the mark. One lady testified,

'I have been so sick but I just want to thank God for giving me the strength to keep going to the gardens and cooking when my lazy, good-for-nothing husband refuses to lift a finger to help me'. Of course, the husband wished that he have could disappear into thin air, especially when most of the other women turned and glared at him. We had to explain to the people that this time was set aside to tell about what God was doing and not what their partners were *not* doing. We hoped that the Bible's teaching on how men must love their wives as Jesus loves the church and sacrificed himself for it, would bring about change in their relationships, and for many, it certainly did.

- 31 -
BETTY'S STORY OF LITTLE ISRAEL

> Why are you cast down, O my soul, and why are you in turmoil within me? Hope in God, for I shall again praise him, my salvation and my God.
>
> PSALM 42:11

John and I (Betty) had just returned from the Sunday morning meeting of the new Tugutil believers. Most were still relatively young Christians, having not all that long ago heard the Gospel message and trusted in Christ. I settled our five month old son, Matthew, down for his nap and was preparing lunch for John and the girls and John's mum who was visiting us in the jungles of Halmahera. We had just returned from our eleven month furlough in Australia and, during that time, John's dad had passed away and our beautiful little boy Matthew was born. When the time came to return to Lili, we insisted Mum return with us and stay on for a month. She loved life in Lili and the tribal people loved her so much that we extended her time with us to four months.

But the quiet of that Sunday was about to be shattered. We all heard the panicked young tribal mother calling out as she hurried up the jungle path towards our home. Her five month old daughter, Ongo Israel, was strapped to her front in a dirty sarong. 'Ongo' is the female marker in the language and 'Israel' was the name given to her daughter after the family heard about God's chosen people, Israel. Most of the babies born after hearing the Bible narrative were given Biblical names but the name 'Israel' was not politically correct in a Muslim majority nation. Her baby was experiencing significant abdominal discomfort. Little Ongo Israel was far from well. The baby pulled her knees up to her abdomen and screamed in agony as a spasm of pain overwhelmed her. Being a nurse, I asked the concerned young mother questions about the child's condition. It quickly became obvious that the baby was deteriorating as the spasms increased in severity and frequency. A call on the SSB radio to the base in Ambon revealed that the Indonesian doctor who had been so helpful to us in the past was presently unavailable.

I cradled the little one as yet another spasm overwhelmed the baby's fragile frame.

'Don't cry darling. Mummy's here,' I said to the precious child, realising with surprise that I was talking to the baby in English as if she were my own. But my baby was safely sound asleep in his cot.

Ongo Israel's Mummy and Daddy were sitting there, desperately concerned about the plight of their longed-for little daughter that God had so graciously given to them after a number of miscarriages. So, as the wait began for the doctor in town to get back to us, I administered antibiotics to the baby as a precautionary measure. The whole family moved into our home as the wait continued. Finally, after 36 hours filled with great anxiety and a growing feeling of helplessness, the radio crackled into life with a request from the doctor to perform a test on the baby. I immediately did the test and reported back the result. A bowel obstruction was the diagnosis given and an immediate evacuation to a large hospital strongly recommended if the baby was to have any chance of survival. Surgery would have to be performed immediately. The doctor recommended we continue with the antibiotic medicine and we gave it to little Israel, who opened her mouth eagerly like a baby bird receiving food.

How would we tell the desperate parents that their little one had to be flown out to a place where they would have to cut her open and try to fix what was wrong? In Tugutil thinking, the only reason you cut someone open is to kill them. I also had to warn them that even if they agreed to the surgery, there was no guarantee that Ongo Israel would survive. Their immediate agreement to our proposal indicated both their extreme feelings of desperation and their trust and confidence in us. But we were feeling anything but confident in the whole situation.

Now we had to find the money to call in the mission plane to fly her out for the desperately needed surgery. We had saved some money to pay for a trip to visit our girls away at mission school. These were the only funds we had to cover the costs. But it seemed a relatively small price to pay for the life of a child, although it did cause a little stab of pain (followed by guilt) as I struggled to come to grips with the fact that once again I would not see our girls for a full four months once they left for school after the Christmas holidays.

But all of those thoughts had to be put on hold for the emergency at hand. Having John's elderly mum with us meant that, if she was willing, she could remain in the tribe with Naomi and Anita, allowing John, Matthew and myself to take the baby and her mother to hospital. Without any hesitation she agreed with the plan and with the girls very comfortable in the language and our neighbours nearby, we were confident that they would be fine.

THE TUGUTIL

So this young Tugutil mum who had only ever worn minimal clothing and never any footwear, prepared to travel out of the jungle for the first time. She had never used a toilet and had never travelled on any vehicle, let alone flown in a plane, but she bravely gathered her baby, a few pieces of clothing and some sandals we were able to find for her and stepped onto our little mission plane. Ongo Israel's daddy said his good-byes to his little girl and promptly left to go hunting in the jungle to help pass the tense hours as he waited for news. John, Matthew and I completed the group of passengers on the plane. As quickly as possible our wonderful pilot, Dave Huntting, had us in the air and on our way to the hospital.

Two and a half hours later we landed at the airport in Ambon and were quickly rushed to the hospital in our business manager's vehicle. All of this was thoroughly terrifying to the young mother, who had never seen traffic, buildings or built-up areas in her life before. But she was so focused on the task at hand that she refused to allow any of these extreme former unknowns to daunt her in her goal to do everything to help her baby.

X-rays soon confirmed the diagnosis that the doctor had given over the radio. Everything had to be translated for Ongo Israel's mum, who spoke only her tribal tongue, with no understanding of Indonesian. The one and only surgeon on Ambon – an island with a population of over 200,000 - was unable to operate until late that night. After excessively long hours in theatre, he had to get some rest before attempting such a surgery. Every minute, let alone hour, was vital if little Israel was to have any chance of surviving. Her little belly, by this stage, was hugely distended and she was in constant agony and, by this time, was also running a fever. But what else could be done? These kinds of medical emergencies are sad realities of life for those living in the more remote parts of the country.

Ongo Israel was admitted to hospital and we were instructed to try to locate and purchase a catheter small enough to perform the task of emptying the baby's bladder. It was our responsibility to locate and purchase things like this from the city's pharmacies, along with any medication prescribed for treating Ongo Israel post-operatively. The hospital doesn't automatically supply these medications or equipment. In that environment there is no treatment for pain and no attempts were made to lower the fever. Despite this, I did all that I possibly could to make her as comfortable as possible. As the wait continued, our son Matthew also began to run a high fever. He had been left in the care of other missionaries living in town and we immediately suspected malaria.

Our son Matthew as a baby in Lili

Finally, at 9.45 p.m., surgery began. Fifty-six hours had elapsed since little Israel had been brought to our door. Things were not looking good but much prayer back in Lili was being poured out to our great God, the Master Healer. We were able to see her briefly post-operatively before she was taken to the hospital's Intensive Care Unit. The surgeon took time to convey what he had done and his hope that she was going to make it. He informed us that she would need to remain in the hospital for ten days. We translated all this to Israel's mum. After the gruelling wait, our hopes were renewed and we were greatly encouraged by this positive prognosis. We returned to the mission's Guesthouse to sink into exhausted sleep. I was relieved to be able to feed and care for my own baby, Matthew, who continued to run high fevers. Suspecting malaria, the decision was made for John to take him to the doctor the next day.

Early that next morning we received an unexpected phone call from our dear friend David Evans. He knew nothing about the situation we were going through but had felt compelled to call Ambon and check on how the Sharpe's were going. Not expecting us to even be in Ambon, thinking we would still be in Lili, he was amazed to hear John answer his call. It was wonderful that Dave was able to get through, as the phone connection between Australia and Ambon was often unpredictable in those days.

John quickly filled Dave in on the situation regarding Ongo Israel. He assured us of his, and his wife Sandra's prayers along with those of our home church. He was sure the church would help us cover the flight expenses involved in this emergency which they subsequently did. This surprise contact with a dear friend from home was indeed a huge comfort and reminder that God was caring for us through His people.

At 8 o'clock that morning a second phone call came from the hospital, shattering all illusions of a physical healing for little Israel. She was not doing well and the staff advised us to bring her mother up immediately. Upon our arrival, the staff rushed us to Israel's bedside. Her veins had collapsed and they could not get an Intravenous drip in to hydrate the little one. She looked so frail and sweet. Her tummy was no longer distended.

The nursing staff urged her mother, Goloko, to feed her. Goloko put her to the breast and little Israel sucked strongly. She must have been so comforted to be once again in her Mummy's arms after having been through so much. After sucking so strongly the staff insisted she stop and rest, and they ushered us out of the room. Just a couple of minutes later they came out to say that little Israel had died.

How do you translate that to the mother who was unable to comprehend that her God-given little girl who had just sucked so strongly at her breast was now gone? We went back into the room and Goloko took her dead baby into her arms and began to wail. As we looked around the intensive care room, it was devastating to see the lack of equipment in the room where Israel had spent her last night. At a time when she needed the latest medical equipment and sterile conditions, all she'd had was this poorly equipped room containing a couple of beds, an oxygen bottle and an air conditioner.

Again guilt ripped through my mind as I wondered whether things might have been different if I had insisted on staying with the baby through the night. I wondered if, perhaps, this might have increased her chances of surviving post-operatively. But now it was all too late.

Goloko continued to wail loudly and would not let go of her baby as staff, fearing that she would upset other patients, tried to keep her quiet and arrange Israel's little body. We became aware as Goloko wailed that she was singing to her dead baby and lamenting the fact that Israel would never see her brothers, her Daddy or her home again and that they would never see her. I quietly suggested to her that they would see each other in Heaven. Goloko then began to sing a new song to her baby proclaiming her solid hope of eternal life. Finally, I was able to talk Goloko into laying her precious bundle on the bed so that the nurses could straighten out her fragile little limbs.

Meanwhile, John began frantically organising the mission plane to fly us all back to our jungle home that afternoon and to get Matthew to the doctor one more time before we left. As we were leaving, the hospital anaesthetist told us that the surgery had in fact not gone well at all and that the surgeon had failed to remove all the gangrenous portions of bowel. Therefore it was inevitable that Israel was going to die. The surgeon had told us what he knew we wanted to hear, rather than conveying the full gravity of the situation. How discouraged and betrayed we felt! Why had our hopes been raised only to be dashed the very next day? Where was God in all this? We had thanked God only ten hours earlier, believing that He had been instrumental in what we thought was going to be a wonderful outcome. It almost felt like God had betrayed us, such was our disappointment and sadness over what had just taken place. These young Tugutil parents had only been Christians for such a short time and we wondered how this would affect their newfound faith in God. But the Lord sees the big picture and in His infinite wisdom, He will do that which is right, even if at the time we have difficulty understanding what's going on. Amazingly, wonderfully, Ongo Israel's death did nothing to diminish her parents' faith in the God whom they had recently come to know and trust.

So back to our jungle home we flew. How surreal that journey was! In our little six-seater mission plane was a mother with her dearly beloved dead baby daughter, and another mother with her dearly beloved baby son, sick but still very much alive. As we sat side by side for the two and a half hour flight home, it all seemed so unfair and it made me feel so guilty. I knew that had it been my child that was so sick we would have spared no expense and flown her to the capital city of Indonesia, or even back home to

Australia, where there were much better-equipped hospitals and highly trained staff.

Arriving back at our jungle airstrip, Goloko handed her little bundle to me as she got down from the plane and fell into the loving, caring arms of other believers, who by now were all wailing along with her. As I negotiated getting out of the plane with the dead little baby, I looked up and my heart sank. There was one of baby Israel's uncles, Puhuhu's son-in-law who, along with his witchdoctor uncle, had so violently opposed our teaching of the Gospel. He began yelling abuse at me. It was then that the ladies' wailing, the deeply emotionally draining time we'd had, and his tirade against me suddenly all became too much.

'Why are you crying?' the uncle taunted. 'We don't cry when we kill a pig and the lumber company people didn't cry when they killed one of our people up in the jungle, so why are you crying when you have killed this little baby?' I looked around for Goloko to take her baby from my arms but I couldn't see her. As John hurriedly assisted the pilot to refuel the plane so he could return to Ambon before the airport's 6 pm curfew, I walked off the airstrip and up the long road that would take me to the house of Israel's aunt and someone who could take charge of the little baby's body. Now the uncle was walking along beside me, angry and abusive, still yelling threats while holding his razor sharp machete, standard equipment for Tugutil men when travelling. On the other side was a young Christian man, Habiana, softly speaking words of encouragement and urging me to say nothing and just remain quiet. This was obviously the right course of action in this potentially volatile situation. As I walked, I realised this would be the last time I would ever hold that dear little one in my arms. As the long walk came to an end at the aunt's house, I laid the baby down on the bark floor and left. I continued my walk back to our house further inland and really have no memory of that lonely walk home.

Matthew continued to run high fevers for five more days and then, suddenly, they stopped. The funeral for baby Israel was held the next day and we wondered whether members of the uncle's family who had also opposed the Gospel may take matters further. Work and life resumed quickly, with no time to process the enormity of what we had gone through. Israel's father was so very supportive and protective of us, defending me to his brother and warning him to cease his verbal abuse or else. Christmas Day was upon us just a few days later.

A week or so after that John left for a three week leadership trip around the country. I continued on with my medical work among the tribal people, feeling more and more overwhelmed as the days, weeks, months rolled by. I lived in dread of another medical crisis such as the one we had just experienced with little Israel. My fears that another life and death situation would arise were realised just a week after John had left to go on his leadership trip. It threatened to be my undoing but I stubbornly refused to give in to all the emotions churning inside. I just kept pressing on with no hope of relief, feeling terribly alone. Working among these people certainly had a traumatic side and I struggled not to take personal responsibility for the survival of every person who came to me with medical problems. Despite the tragedies we encountered, we also saw many people survive potentially fatal illnesses and accidents from which they would have had no chance of recovering without our assistance. Sadly, illness, injury and death were an all-too familiar part of life for these people we had come to love so dearly.

- 32 -
SINGING, A WONDERFUL NEW EXPERIENCE FOR THE TUGUTIL

> Oh sing to the Lord a new song; sing to the Lord, all the Earth!
>
> PSALM 96:1

Living among the Tugutil people gave us a good insight into what tribal life was actually like for the people. The longer we were there, the more we discovered how terribly hard their quest for survival actually was. This had become more obvious as we discovered the system of food laws and other taboos that existed within the culture. One of these taboos forbade the singing of songs, a rule that denied them the God-given enjoyment of music and singing. For the Tugutil, singing had been replaced with one simple chant which they believed was the only form of 'music' that the spirits permitted. We did hear simple stories being put to the few notes of the chant sometimes, but absolutely no other songs were allowed. Often as the people passed by our homes, they would hear music coming from our cassette players, so they certainly had some exposure to these melodies even though they couldn't understand any of the English or Indonesian lyrics.

At the completion of our teaching in the evangelism phase, and with most of the people now expressing faith in Christ, we explained how they could express their praise and thanks to God through prayer or simply telling God what was in their hearts. We told them that many believers around the world convey their thanks and praise to God through music. Through songs, they too could express the thankfulness in their hearts to God or sing about wonderful truths from the Bible. We played recordings of some of the songs written by the new Christians in Taliabu, another tribal group that had recently been reached by our colleagues in another part of the province. Immediately, the request came for us to translate the Taliabu words. They wanted us to teach them the songs so that they too could sing praises to God.

Having heard reports out of Taliabu of the believers' excitement as they wrote and developed their own praise music, we resisted the temptation to expedite the introduction of music. Instead, we told them that they could sing a new song to the Lord and that God had placed a new song in their hearts. Therefore, we explained, they should write their own music and lyrics that reflected their love and adoration of God. These songs would be so much more meaningful than songs given to them by us. Thus began the process of these new believers writing their own lyrics and then coming up with accompanying tunes through which they could praise God in song.

The very first song they wrote was titled *O Yesusu dika Wapoa* or 'Only Jesus Was Able'. Because it was a very long lyric, and because the tune sounded similar to a funeral dirge, it took forever to sing. We quickly let them know that it is okay to create much shorter songs and that they didn't need to fit the entire Bible into just one song. We encouraged them to write songs that contained just one or two aspects of what Jesus did. We showed them that they could sing about how we should now live as Christians in

SINGING, A WONDERFUL NEW EXPERIENCE FOR THE TUGUTIL

light of the Gospel. Thus more and more songs, and better songs, began to be written by the people. No doubt God was just as pleased with their earlier efforts because they worshipped Him from the heart.

Aware of what had happened in Taliabu, a Christian musicologist from the US decided that he would like to visit that tribe and, when he heard that a similar thing was happening in Lili, he added us to his itinerary. Upon arrival, he was astounded to find that the Tugutil had worked out for themselves how to sing four part harmonies, something unheard of among singers and songwriters who had never had any kind of training, as far as he was concerned. He also had the people make panpipes from the bamboo found in the jungle and in the two weeks he was with us, he taught them not only to play the panpipes to their tunes, but also how to write down the notes they were playing. Here was another instance of us being astounded by the amazing intellects of many of these incredible people with whom we had the privilege of living.

Because drums played a big part in calling the spirits, in the minds of the Tugutil any musical association with a drum beat pattern was considered unacceptable and rejected as part of their old life. On one occasion O Life (pronounced Lee Fay), a prolific song writer, wrote a fantastic lyric about how God brought the Children of Israel out of Egypt. But each line of these lyrics contained a few too many words to be carried by the kinds of tunes they had been coming up with. Really wanting to see this new song added to their ever-growing song book, I played around with it and came up with a tune that seemed to work well, despite the lengthy lines in the song. The tune had quite a traditional Jewish sound to it and a great beat. I certainly thought it was really good, in fact probably the best song thus far. Life and some of the young guys tried to learn it and I was wondering when they would introduce it to the church. My answer came in no uncertain terms when some of the older men approached Life and told him to tell me that my tune sounded "just like it had come straight from Satan." What a rebuff! Well, needless to say, that was the beginning and the very abrupt end to my involvement in any song writing for the Tugutil Church! Actually, I really didn't mind, knowing that they should be the ones writing songs that best represented their expression of praise and worship to God. They certainly have continued their song writing, writing some wonderful songs. The people loved gathering together to sing - something they had believed they could never do, prior to the coming of the Gospel.

Anita Miles developed a literacy program and trained literacy teachers. Later, the people wrote and sang their own songs

- 33 -
ETANGA'S STORY

> Always be prepared to make a defence to anyone who asks you for a reason for the hope that is in you; yet do it with gentleness and respect.
>
> 1 PETER 3:15B

Ongo Etanga was a girl of about six or seven years of age when we first entered the tribe in 1982. She usually sported a cheery smile whenever we met, despite the very hard life that seemed par for the course for young tribal girls. She loved coming to the missionaries' houses where she would play with our children, with whom she was forming close friendships. As the teaching of the Bible began, Etanga's little world was confronted with a message that was about to radically change her worldview and turn her life upside down. Hearing about the God who made everything she saw around her, she marvelled at the incredible power of someone who could, simply by speaking, bring everything into existence.

Finally the day came when Etanga heard the story of the life of Jesus which culminated in His death on the cross and His resurrection. She now understood that Jesus had done everything necessary to put her right with God if she would only trust in Him and His finished, saving work. This she had enthusiastically done, along with many others, even during the teaching of the

Old Testament lessons when they knew Him only as the Promised Redeemer.

Shortly after becoming a newborn babe in Christ, Etanga one day entered the jungle and collected a large number of canari nuts that had fallen from huge trees dotted throughout the jungle. Once she had gathered enough nuts, she would then make the long walk to a village up north where a Chinese trader would pay her for them. With the money she had previously saved, this transaction would give her sufficient money to purchase the new sarong that she so desperately needed.

Arriving at the small trading store in the village three hours walk to our north, Etanga proceeded to transact her business. But as important as that business was, young Etanga now had something even more important on her mind. *Did the trader, a man called Pak Sin, know and understand God's wonderful story of redemption?* The Tugutil knew that they were often looked down upon by the village people and, being a female and a child to boot, Etanga had every reason to just keep quiet and not draw any attention to herself.

But no, Etanga wanted to be sure that this man - who incidentally, was a deacon in the village church - knew exactly what Jesus had done for him.

'Pak Sin', she called to get his attention. 'If you died today, would you go to Heaven or to Hell? He thought for a moment and replied,

'Well child, it depends on whether I have done more good things than bad things. In that case I would go to Heaven but if I'd done more bad things than good things, then I'd go to Hell.' Etanga thought about his response and then replied.

'Pak Sin. If it is true that we can get to Heaven by doing more good things than bad things, then can you please explain to me why Jesus, God's Son, had to come to this Earth, live His perfect life and then die that horrible and terribly cruel death on that cross. Please tell me Pak Sin, if we can do it ourselves then why did God have to send His Son?' Pak Sin had no response to this brave child's insightful question, which revealed that she clearly understood the truth that he had failed to grasp - that Jesus alone is God's means of redemption.

- 34 -
THE FIRST BAPTISMS

> Go therefore and make disciples of all nations, baptising them in the name of the Father and of the Son and of the Holy Spirit.
>
> MATTHEW 28:19

As we presented the Gospel to the Tugutil people, we went to great lengths to ensure that they clearly understood that salvation was *by grace alone through faith*. Animistic people live their lives continually doing things to appease and manipulate the Spirits. We wanted to avoid the possibility of them ever thinking they could approach God in that way. The evangelistic approach we used purposefully excluded their participation in anything that could possibly be interpreted as a meritorious work and therefore seen as grounds for salvation. Throughout the six months of evangelistic teaching they heard over and over again how God declared men righteous, based on repentance and their faith in Him and His Word. Therefore, we were reluctant to immediately highlight baptism as something they should undergo as believers. We waited until the subject naturally occurred again as we taught through the book of Acts.

When the doctrine of believers' baptism was introduced, the team went to great lengths to emphasise its symbolism in showing our identification with Christ's death, burial and resurrection. The people were told that, just as Jesus had died, was buried and then rose three days later from the dead, as far as God was concerned, all who were 'in Christ' had also died, were buried and had risen to new life. Their own baptism would act this out and declare its wonderful truth to all present. It wasn't long before some of the first group of believers, having heard the teaching on baptism, requested that they be baptised.

The first baptism would take place after Sunday morning church in the nearby Lili River. In discussing the upcoming event with our Indonesian co-worker, Chris Lahu, it came out that some of the people had understood our teaching on baptism to mean that, just as Jesus was crucified and then resurrected after three days in the grave, so, in acting this out, they would have to remain under the water for three days! Just as God had raised Jesus after three days, so they believed that He would also raise them up. Chris immediately corrected their misunderstanding and explained in detail what would actually happen, ensuring that everybody understood it correctly this time!

Besides being surprised that the Tugutil hadn't connected the event to what we had taught about John's baptism and the baptism of Jesus, we were once again totally blown away by the degree to

THE FIRST BAPTISMS

which they were willing to trust God. If God required them to remain under the water for three days, then that was enough for them. Jesus was their Maker who had wonderfully saved them and His Word was to be believed and acted upon. To these Tugutil believers, there was no better place to be than right in the centre of His will, whatever the cost.

Our son Matthew accompanied me on one visit back to Lili and was baptised by church leaders in the Lili River

- 35 -
REFLECTING ON THE EXPERIENCE

> O Lord, you have searched me and known me! ... and are acquainted with all my ways.
>
> PSALM 139:1, 3

It is difficult to put an exact figure on how many of the Tugutil people trusted Christ by the time we completed the story. Certainly the vast majority came to faith during that time or soon after as the story was told over and over again by their own people. It seemed that many had decided early on, when hearing the Old Testament stories, that what they were hearing was true and that God and His promises should be fully trusted. Since that time, their own people have taken over the storytelling work, improving it by using better key biblical terms and better cultural illustrations. These folk have gone to other Tugutil areas on Halmahera Island, resulting in the establishment of other Tugutil churches. The very first outreach involved Don and Heather, along with an outstanding young tribal couple, Meusu and Sipora, moving to another area and planting a church some distance to the north of Lili. God has raised up some wonderful leaders who, along with their families, have willingly put their lives on the line to see a number of new areas reached with the Gospel.

THE TUGUTIL

The most severe testing of the church came in 1998 when fighting erupted between Muslims and Christians in Ambon, eventually spreading throughout the entire province. Stories emerged of attacks carried out against the Christians in Lili along with news of how God miraculously thwarted each attack. During those turbulent years, which saw thousands of people killed in the province, not one Tugutil person was killed or even injured. Just as God protected us from the Tugutil people themselves in those early days, He in turn protected them from the Jihad warriors who sought to drive them from their land and destroy them.

But to merely mention the amazing stories that form part of this account of God's grace among the Tugutil and fail to mention the things I would now do very differently would be remiss of me. Life for me, with my "sanguine-phlegmatic" temperament, usually involves very little time spent in reflecting on the past, especially if it involves some of my mistakes. Of course, the major downside of little time spent in reflection is that it can lead to the repeating of those same old blunders over and over again. So, in compelling myself to reflect on those years, I've come up with some things that I hope I would do very differently if we were again heading off to bring the gospel to an unreached people group.

One area of difference between Betty and me centred on taking holidays. Living in Lili certainly involved many stress-filled days and my wife longed for breaks and the chance to just chill, away from all the pressures. On the other hand, I coped much better with the stress and, considering the anxiety created by travelling in and out of Lili by boat, simply thought it better to just stay put unless we absolutely had to go out. On the surface, Betty's frequent seasickness helped in convincing her that my approach was indeed the right one. When the plane service did eventually come, it was often the expense that made me reluctant to spend even more money on travelling in and out of the jungle. Going some place nice for a holiday within the country just wasn't going to happen and if we did go somewhere, it would be to visit Naomi and Anita far away at school in another province. If I'd had the good sense to perceive the importance of Betty's need for refreshing breaks (and probably my own need as well) I feel I could have better supported her in light of the huge pressure she carried with the medical program. In hindsight, I would have ensured that those kinds of trips happened. We all need to have our batteries recharged. We married folk need to build times of rest and enjoyment into our marriages and family times which so often yield precious memories. Most of that time, I failed to realise the immense emotional load Betty carried and the trauma she endured when people were dangerously ill or had passed away. These days, we try to take regular breaks together.

Another regret I have was that I wasn't far more considerate of Betty's limited energy levels. There were often times when, at the end of the day she would be totally worn out, but during the evenings people would arrive at our house just to talk and kill time. As the group often included a number of women, I would usually encourage Betty to join us. People functioning in this kind of work need to know their limits and work within them if they are going to hang in for the long haul. Spouses need to understand that and be supportive of their partners. Betty has since told me that she often believed that no matter how much she did, it would never be enough to meet what she saw as my excessive expectations. I sure wish I had known then what I do now – as I would have been a lot more considerate of my dear wife.

As mentioned in a previous chapter, my understanding of a

'good missionary' was a person who was willing to make great sacrifices for others. Then came my appointment to leadership in the province and later, to our field leadership committee. These roles only served to further intensify this thinking, as I then felt the pressure to lead by example and of course, applied my 'great sacrifices' model to the family as well. It seemed there was always just so much to do -especially with leadership responsibilities also thrown into the mix. Consequently, it was often my family that drew the short straw. Getting the family and work balance just right is so much easier said than done, and the nature of missionary work often demanded our full attention for sustained periods of time. But if that state of frantic busyness always characterises our lives, then we stand guilty of neglecting our families, something God hates. We must certainly never confuse busyness with spirituality, something that unfortunately is a common error in western Christianity.

I remember that after returning to Australia, Betty and I were invited to a marriage enrichment weekend. Someone else had covered the cost so I thought, *Why not? Even if we don't really need it.* Betty, on the other hand, was thrilled when she heard of this opportunity. She obviously had a far more realistic appreciation of where things were at in our marriage than I did. It was during that weekend that I discovered what a poor job I did of really listening to my wife. Being forced to use the skill of reflective listening sure exposed that! I remember at the time thinking how doing a course like that before going overseas would have been incredibly helpful. But simply doing a course doesn't guarantee that you will put it all into practice. People who live and work together in isolated contexts really do need to be able to communicate well and be especially good listeners. Those very same skills are also essential among team members and would help teams avoid many of the misunderstandings that can so easily destroy their unity.

But my final reflection addresses a question which we have often been asked. Knowing what you know now, and having gone through what you did, would you do it all again? Without hesitation, my answer is *yes!* Before we began, it was definitely due to the mercy of God that we had no idea of all that would lie ahead of us. Pulling these stories together into one book has left me amazed as I relive and reflect on the things we and our dear co-workers went through. But again, it simply highlights the fact that God does give His sustaining grace to us for each situation as it happens, and it is that grace that carries you through. If we were to do it all again, I hope we would function a lot smarter in some ways and now, being a lot more aware missiologically, I would want to do a couple of things in the area of the church planting just a little differently. An example of this would be to include the new Christians in any discussions we had as a team in any areas that concerned the church. There they hopefully would have seen us model how biblical eldership works. It would also reinforce the peoples' ownership and responsibility as new members of our team, to see their church nurtured and growing in their love for God.

Our departure from the tribe. Even Puhuhu came to say goodbye

THE TUGUTIL

But as to the impact our team had on the Tugutil people, and how God used us among them, we can only be filled with thankfulness and praise. The experience certainly allowed us the rare privilege of seeing God at work - transforming a totally unreached group of people who had heard absolutely nothing of the message of the Bible. The apostle Paul said in the book of Romans,

'I make it my ambition to preach the Gospel, not where Christ has already been named, lest I build on someone else's foundation, but as it is written, those who have never been told of him will see, and those who have never heard will understand.'

God's Spirit gave that group of people who had never heard of Him miraculous understanding. It was He who changed them into a people who now see themselves as incredibly loved and ever so highly valued by their Creator God. His love for them is so immense that He sent His only Son, Jesus Christ, to die an agonising death in their place so that they could become His sons and daughters. Yes, despite the personal cost involved, it certainly was worth doing - knowing that God used it to produce beautiful Tugutil fruit that will last for eternity!

Naomi and Anita were able to visit their
friends prior to returning to Australia

REFLECTING ON THE EXPERIENCE

Returning to Lili to visit the people. The Tugutil we first met were totally undemonstrative when it came to showing any affection and there was no way a woman would hug someone of the opposite sex. Just look at them now!

About the Authors

John and Betty Sharpe and their family served in Indonesia from 1980 – 1995. During that time they worked as part of a cross-cultural missionary team to the Tugutil People from 1982 to the end of 1991. Their involvement with Field leadership then saw them moved to Ambon, the Provincial capital of Maluku where they served out the remainder of their time in Indonesia. Since returning to Australia they have remained involved in missions and currently work with Crossview Australia in Sydney.

Contact John and Betty: thetugutil@gmail.com

Training Resources for Making Truth Accessible

Providing Biblical resources for people who want to know more about Christ and grow in the Lord. Our communication, culture and language learning, church planting and discipleship resources equip people to be more effective as they serve in cross-cultural contexts, either locally or globally.

Find more resources at
accesstruth.com

www.ingramcontent.com/pod-product-compliance
Lightning Source LLC
Chambersburg PA
CBHW032039290426
44110CB00012B/869